D1745451

GOD's GRACE & HUMAN HEALTH

J. HAROLD ELLENS

Nashville / Abingdon

GOD'S GRACE AND HUMAN HEALTH

Copyright © 1982 by Abingdon

Library of Congress Cataloging in Publication Data

ELLENS, J. HAROLD, 1932–
    God's grace and human health.
    Bibliography: p.
    Includes index.
    1. Holistic medicine. 2. Medicine—Philosophy. 3. Psychology,
Religious. 4. Grace (Theology) I. Title.
R723.E45   150'.19'0882   82-3931   AACR2

ISBN 0-687-15326-3

Manufactured by the Parthenon Press at
Nashville, Tennessee, United States of America

Contents

This book is for **Deborah Lynn Ellens,** my eldest daughter. Her vigorously thoughtful and persistently inquiring mind expressed with courageously authentic spirit has illumined and, at some crucial points, corrected my theological understanding.

* * * *

I wish to acknowledge with sturdy gratitude the generosity of my dear friend **Professor Doctor William John Murray Janson,** Professor of Pastoral Psychology at the University of South Africa at Pretoria. He read the page proofs with great skill and precision and prepared the index. He is, in that sense, an enthusiastic collaborator in this work.

* * * *

The central three chapters were developed as the John G. Finch Lectureship at the Fuller Graduate School of Theology for 1980. Special appreciation should be expressed to **Dr. H. Newton Malony** and **Dr. Neil C. Warren** for the gracious hospitality extended me on that occasion.

Preface

Thinking about human health is a stimulating and mystifying matter. It stimulates the mind, drawing one into the marvelous scope and variety of human life and function as one begins to realize that the issue of health touches and takes in most of the experience of being human. It is immediately apparent not only that one must always be either healthy or unhealthy in body, mind, and psyche, but also there are an incredible number and quality of ways in which one can be sick or well. Yet, it is impressive that those ways in which humans get sick tend to fall into very stereotyped patterns. From that point of view, the number and variety of ways people can be pathological seems finite, typical, and relatively predictable. On the other hand, we all have our own individualized style of being ill or well, that is, of reacting to or managing or carrying our health and/or our illness. We are so typically human and yet so surprisingly unique, for better or for worse, in sickness and in health. Likewise getting well can usually be achieved in surprisingly prescribed ways, yet each human does it with an intriguing distinctiveness. That is why it is also mystifying to speak of human health. Humans are or are not healthy so remarkably variously; and as if that did not sufficiently complicate the matter of what health is and how it is achieved, the variety of *definitions* of health in professional literature and in the popular mind is legion.

I remember I was fourteen when I first came genuinely to grips with the issue of what health is. It was during my sophomore year in high school. The quest was stimulated by a rather wide-ranging course in general biology. I was a small, rather neurotic, withdrawn, intense, anxiety laden, shy, pubescent boy, obviously, and at least semiconsciously, maturing extremely late. I am not certain whether the painfulness of body and psyche that seemed to dominate my experience is typical for early adolescence, whether it was mainly physical or psychological, or whether it was healthy at the time. What I do remember is that it stimulated my thinking about health at the same time that it mystified me.

The quest came rather quickly to something helpful: an applied definition of health. I have no idea which supplemental text we were using. It may have been one of those weekly student journals so popular at the time. In any case, it simply said that health is the state or condition in which a person can carry out a normal pattern or program of work without experiencing inappropriate pain. The teacher was impressed that I had caught that. I was astonished that no other student had. The teacher was suffering from a chronic illness, and the other students were rather beyond puberty. Perhaps need prompted me to fix on the issue, which for others was routine.

Since then, I have found that two things are true about health. First, most of us take it for granted when we have it. Second, this elementary definition is the best place to begin thinking about health. In this day of increasing emphasis upon holistic health care, the old positivist notion that health is essentially, if not exclusively, a matter of physical well-being seems to be receding. Few professionals would now argue with the notion that health is more than physical well-being, involving also the interrelatedness of physical, mental, and social well-being. Even in the popular mind the holistic notion is genuinely gaining ground. These gains have been a long time in developing.

In ancient societies of the Near East from 3200 B.C. to A.D.1000—the cultures from which the West draws its sources and resources—Egyptian, Mesopotamian, Hebrew, Greek, and Roman—the stress was on physical well-being and prescriptions for physical hygiene. Matters that would be referred to today as mental hygiene or psychotherapy were largely relegated to the realm of religion. Emphasis upon physical health continued through the Renaissance and well into the eighteenth century. Horace Mann, first secretary of the board of education in the United States, emphasized as late as 1840 that educating for health as physical well-being was crucial. In 1850 A. M. Shattuck in his "Report of the Sanitary Conditions in Massachusetts" emphasized the need for preventive programs of disease control, indicating that health was more than the absence of disease. However, his orientation remained essentially shaped by the physical emphasis.

There were notable exceptions to this over the centuries. Already in Homeric times Asklepios, and more pronouncedly Hippocrates in fifth century Athens, placed considerable emphasis upon both physical and spiritual well-being, that is, the health of *soma* and *psyche*. This emphasis is weaker in the Roman, Galen. In the early modern period it raises its head briefly. John Locke considered "a sound mind in a sound body" to be essential.

It was only after the two world wars of the twentieth century that notions of health as optimal well-being in body, mind, and relationships began to take palpable form. Out of that development came such definitions as the following.

1. Health is a state of complete physical, mental, and social well-being and not merely the absence of disease or infirmity.

2. Health is that complete fitness of body, soundness of mind, and wholeness of emotions that make possible the highest quality of effective living and service.
3. Health is the quality, resulting from the total functioning of the individual, that empowers him to achieve a personally satisfying and socially useful life.
4. Health is the condition under which the individual is able to mobilize all his resources—intellectual, emotional, and physical—for optimum living.

Such holistic axioms take seriously the health-impacting significance of total personhood and do not underestimate the role that social relationships play in enhancing or defeating health. Dr. R. Dunn has claimed quite correctly that at mid-century the goal of health calls for not only the cure or alleviation of disease. It calls for even more than prevention of disease. Rather it looks beyond, to strive for maximum physical, mental, and social efficiency for the individual, for his family, and for the community.

The value of this perspective, as is being generally recognized today, lies in the fact that it considers health in positive rather than negative terms. Health is not merely disease control, cure, or prevention. It is the achievement of a high level of wellness. Health is dynamic process, not static state. It is a life quality into which humans grow on a continuum that reaches ever forward and upward, rather than a status which people can achieve and at which they can then lie dormant or quiescent. Hence it becomes less significant to speak of being healthy or unhealthy and more meaningful to speak of relative levels of wellness or well-being. Physical, mental, and social well-being interact causatively and dynamically on the continuum from minimal to optimal wellness, as seen by most professionals and laity in the helping professions today.

A simple and direct link may be seen between the definition

of health I encountered in 1946 and this holistic notion of health. Health as freedom from disease or pain is a notion that has in it the seeds of the definition of health by J. F. Williams. He asserts that health is that quality of life that enables the individual to live most and serve best.[1] Such a quality of life, instead of mere quantity of physical freedom from disease, inevitably includes the holistic concerns of body, mind, and spirit. Williams emphasizes that the health needs of persons correspond to those of nations: vigor, vitality, progress toward a better way of life, and absorption in pursuit of objective causes that enhance growth in quality.

This emphasis on the intricate relationship between health and growth is crucial for understanding the primary concern of this book about God's grace and human health. Since Francis Bacon's revival and elaboration of Aristotle's controlled scientific method, the modern era has thought about nearly everything, especially the exact and applied sciences, in cause-effect terms. That outlook and its inherent confidence in the human ability to identify, analyze, and solve problems in the world of physical reality has been a great boon to the development of health care and the medical sciences.

The techniques for employing the causative perspective in health care have evolved rapidly. The nineteenth century saw a cause-effect model that largely identified a single effect in human health and illness with a single cause, and vice versa. By 1920, following World War I, a second model was in vogue, taking a more comprehensive approach, recognizing the multiplicity of cause-and-effect factors influencing wellness and illness in humans. A solid advance was evident in epidemiology as regards recognition of the interactive forces in the multiple causes and effects. The social ecological model had been born in which disease, for example, was seen to be the result of the condition of the host, the environment, and personal factors. The rise of Freudian psychology, replacing the old "faculty psychology" of the nineteenth century was not insignificant in this development.

Since World War II and the rise of the World Health Organization (WHO), the multiple cause–multiple effect notion of illness and wellness has reached a relatively sophisticated level, taking with great seriousness the role of social, psychological, and physiological phenomena in shaping the health of humans and, incidentally, of most of the higher animals.

By 1970 in the United States, the effects of J. F. Kennedy's emphasis upon the high-level wellness model, implemented by individual responsibility for exercise, nutrition, stress management, and control of harmful substances, was well entrenched. The decade of the 1980s seems to be moving to the predictable consequence of that, namely, an increasing emphasis upon measurement of wellness quality and efforts to calculate the manner and degree to which that is shaped by the environmental and social psychological issues of relationship, self-image, and will. The objective, obviously, is to quantify the variable factors and so enhance control of illness- and wellness-inducing dynamics.

Unfortunately, the recent progress toward a refined and sophisticated recognition of the function of the interactive body-mind-spirit (*soma-psyche*) dynamo in human health has produced a seriously self-defeating side effect: the increasing preoccupation with the occult in some elements of the helping professions. This does not seem to be a fruitful avenue of pursuit for scientific understanding of how humans may achieve optimal wellness. That preoccupation ranges all the way from the mystical manipulations of Ray Stevens from the Walter Reed Wellness Clinic to the psychedelic drug fantasies of Dr. Timothy Leary's pseudo-prophecy.

A considerable advance was made in health care with the recognition of a triad of interacting agents intrinsic to human persons: body, mind, and psyche.

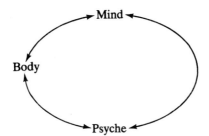

Figure 1.

A substantial step beyond that came with the recognition that a triad of forces extrinsic to human beings also shaped human health: host factors, environmental social factors, and personal behavior factors.

Figure 2. The Social Ecological Model

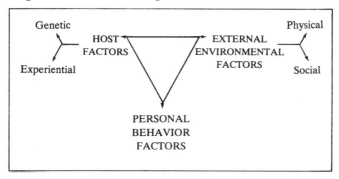

SOURCE: Adapted from J. N. Morris, *Uses of Epidemiology,* 3rd ed. (Edinburgh: Churchill Livingstone, 1975), p. 177.

With the rise of the WHO holistic influence in the world, emphasizing that health is a state of complete physical, mental, and social well-being and not merely the absence of disease or infirmity, the social ecological model was elaborated fully into the environmental health model.

13

Figure 3. The Environment of Health Model

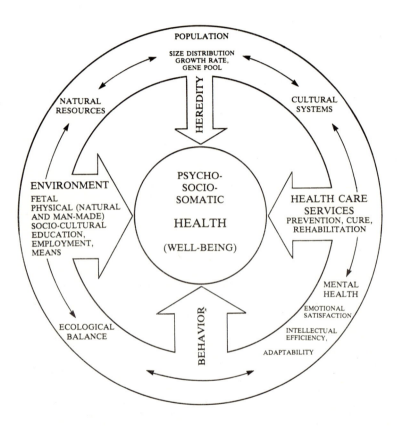

The width of the four large input-to-health arrows indicates assumptions about the relative importance of the inputs to health. The four inputs are shown as relating to and affecting one another by means of an encompassing matrix which could be called the "environment" of the health system.

SOURCE: H. L. Blum, *Planning for Health—Developmental Application of Social Change Theory* (New York: Human Sciences Press, 1974), p. 3.

In this model the holistic emphasis may be defined as concern with the whole person's growth toward intrinsic and extrinsic harmony and homeostasis. It means treating people, not diseases.

Blum, Lalonde, and Dever are now famous for this holistic emphasis, and Granger Westberg urges a variation of it, which he wants to call "wholistic," for what seem insubstantial reasons. Lalonde's term is the health field concept.

Figure 4. The Health Field Concept

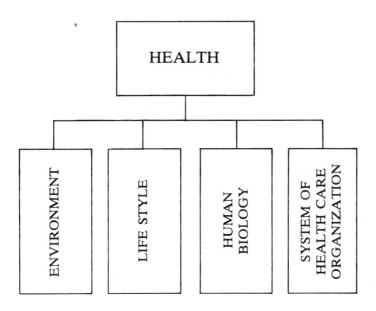

SOURCE: M. Lalonde, *A New Perspective on the Health of Canadians* (Ottawa: Office of the Canadian Minister of National Health and Welfare, April 1974), p. 31.

In figure 5 Dever's model elaborates Lalonde's.

Figure 5. An Epidemiological Model for Health Policy Analysis

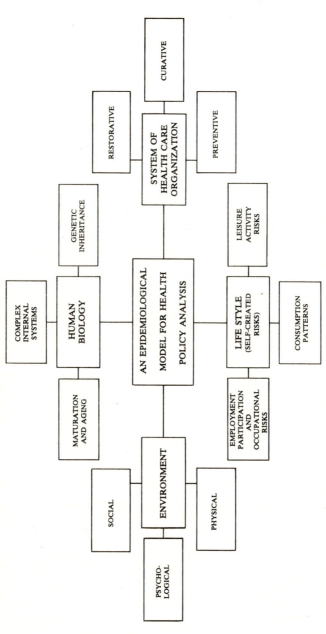

SOURCE: G. E. Alan Dever, "An Epidemiological Model for Health Policy Analysis," *Social Indicators Research* 2, p. 455, 1976. Reprinted by permission from D. Reidel Publishing Company, Dordrecht, Holland.

Thus the matter is carried solidly beyond the notion of health as the cure or elimination of diseases that cause illness. Health is now defined in terms of increasing degrees and conditions of wellness, as indicated in Travis' continuum.

Figure 6. Illness/Wellness Continuum

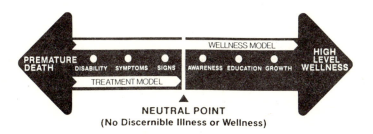

SOURCE: Reprinted with permission from *Wellness Workbook,* by Regina Ryan and John Travis, M.D., published by Ten-Speed Press, 1981.

We have advanced significantly from my insight at fourteen to holistic models. However, already in the notion that health is the state or condition in which a person can carry out a normal pattern or program of work without experiencing inappropriate pain lie the conceptual sources for the comprehensive definition of holistic health.

This book intends to urge one crucial additional dimension to the whole matter: the crucial significance for human health of a person's relationship to God. *God's Grace and Human Health* contends that a person's actual ontological relationship with God, as well as his or her perceived relationship, definitively affects the quality or state of that person's health. Sometimes the "posture before the face of God" is of such a sort that it creates or expands pathology. Sometimes that real or perceived relationship enhances health in body, mind, and/or psyche.

The thesis of this book is not a new invitation to the self-defeating processes of mysticism, parapsychology, spiritism, or the occult. It is very much the opposite. It is a claim for the notion that holistic health involves the self-actualization in persons of the full range of grand potentials for growth in body (*soma*), mind (*nous*), psyche (*psyche*), and spirit (*pneuma*) with which God has invested humans by creating us in his own image.

Health in this book, therefore, must be defined as that state or condition in which a person is achieving or has achieved the quality of life that arises out of a full-orbed realization/actualization of all the physical, spiritual, psychological, and mental possibilities with which God has invested humans and humanness.

The crucial words are, therefore, *growth, dynamics, potential,* and *wellness,* which stand behind and are implied in that definition.

God's Grace and Human Health claims that both the science of the helping professions and the science of theology lead us uniformly to the recognition that the perception and experience of God as a God of grace is the central healing dynamic. There is no magic or mysticism in that. It does not require the peculiarities of the self-limited human fancies of eastern religions. It urges rather a sound rational empirical investigation of measurable and manageable dynamics of the multifaceted human being, functioning spiritually, mentally, psychologically, and physically.

Introduction

During the last five years the American evangelical community has given birth to an important dialogue in the helping professions that is identified as the problem of the integration of psychology and theology. The dialogue demonstrates a serious concern to relate faith to life. On the theoretical level it concerns the question of the essential nature of science. On the practical level it concerns the question of responsible discipleship in applied disciplines. The enterprise seems pregnant with new insights, new routes across the frontiers of the sciences of both theology and psychology, and new potentials for doing both theology and psychology more wisely and creatively at the theoretical and applied levels. The motivation driving the dialogue is the Christian suspicion that there is a necessary, rather than accidental, relationship between being an imager and celebrator of God in his grace, on the one hand, and being a psychological scientist or therapist on the other.

There are difficulties inherent in this matter. One of those is

The original version of this article appeared in *The Bulletin* of CAPS 6:2 (1980) and appears here by permission.

the difficulty of basic definition. In his fine book *Mind and Madness in Ancient Greece,* Bennett Simon declared that the difficulty in talking about psychology is that of getting a commonly agreed upon definition of it, even among the specialists in psychology. Difficulties in definition complicate the evangelical dialogue on integration of psychology and theology considerably. The complexity of summarizing such theoretical constituents of the dialogue as sound theories of personality and pathology is one of the great problems. Achieving a responsible faith-oriented critique and appreciation of classical psychological formulations and models, such as those of Freud, Dreikurs, Adler, Jung, Maslow, Rogers, and Sullivan, is another. This introductory overview addresses (*a*) the central problem, (*b*) two principles, (*c*) eight possibilities, and (*d*) twelve practical applications as a cursory preview of the investigation of God's grace and human health.

There is a central problem in the direction the evangelical dialogue has taken. The problem is rooted in the conceptual model that the name *integration* implies. Models or paradigms are usually difficult to construct. The way faith relates to science, or Christian commitment to psychological theory and practice, is surely far from self-evident.

Dr. Arthur Holmes contends there are three ways science and religion relate.

1. Both use models to explain reality.
2. Conflict is never ultimately over empirical data but regarding a priori principles or philosophical assumptions: faith commitments.
3. Properly conceived all science, as all human experience, finds its ultimate meaning in religion: faith perspective.

Dr. Nicholas Wolterstorff essentially agrees, but presses harder the fact that all scientific theory formulation is born, in the first place, out of one's religious and theological predisposition. All the data one acquires is, therefore, not strictly speaking empirical data or objective rationality but rather the formulations of *Reason Within the Bounds of Religion.*

Both observations help to focus the problematic issue rooted in the name of the conceptual model: *integration.* The model suggests two disparate entities, psychology and theology, essentially alien to each other, which must be lined up or force-fitted to each other in order to insure decent or responsible evangelical work in the helping professions.

This is an epistemological problem on the theoretical science level, a structural problem on the applied science level, and a problem of psychodynamic dissonance on the experience level.

It is a problem because the integration model is an inaccurate picture of reality on two counts. First, it holds at its base the essentially American-Fundamentalist notion that truth comes only through the Christian Scriptures, by the special revealing action of the Holy Spirit of God. Such a view devalues God's general revelation in the world studied by the natural and social sciences. That is, the name *integration* suggests that science, our reading of God's book in nature, is at war with the Christian religion, our reading of God's other book, the Scriptures.

That notion is a residuum of "old-time Fundamentalism" in the schizophrenic way it sets the natural and supernatural worlds at odds, the apocalyptic way it demarcates the domain of God and of the demonic, and the pagan suggestion that lies at the bottom of this dichotomy, i.e. that God does not live here but must invade alien territory to enter the domain of "this world" and its scientific truths. Scholars who stand more consciously in the historic tradition of the Reformation should know very well that God lives here, but in view of their extremely limited contribution to our evangelical dialogue, they give the distinct impression that they are not clearly sure that God's living here really makes that much difference. There are, however, evangelicals of both traditions who are beginning to understand the problem with the integration model and reach beyond it. Benner from Wheaton, Malony from Fuller, Carter from Rosemead, Koteskey from Asbury, Berry from Atlanta, De Graaf from Toronto, and others are beginning to acknowledge the deficiency of the model.

The name of the model is further a problem, because it tends to suggest that effective Christian life in the helping professions requires absorbing psychology into theology or vice versa.

Gary Collins' book *The Rebuilding of Psychology,* which may be credited for focusing the dialogue in 1977, in effect suggests that psychology and theology remain aliens to be aligned but never really integrated, disparate fields to be worked in by individual psychologists and believers, but not quite a place for either to be at home. Insofar as a Christian feels at home in psychology while retaining his faith commitment, he does so by forcing psychological notions into his belief categories and proceeds as though the science of psychology has no prerogatives of its own.

John Carter and Bruce Narramore in *The Integration of Psychology and Theology* insist that one must either have theology absorb psychology or psychology absorb theology. One is either a psychologist who happens incidentally to be a believer and hence a kind of lay theologian, or one is a theologian who happens incidentally to be thoughtful in a kind of popularized psychology.

Koteskey seems to be reaching out for a more legitimate model in *Psychology from a Christian Perspective,* but he needs to write a second book in which he takes more account of the Calvinist theology of sphere sovereignty and escapes the biblicist pietism with which his terminology and his concepts labor. C. Markham Berry, wrote an article in the

Journal of Psychology and Theology for Spring, 1980. He titled it "Approaching the Integration of the Social Sciences and Biblical Theology." In it he formulates the following argument. Both theology and psychology as sciences, are abstractions from the evidence of their data bases. Those abstractions are philosophically shaped. They are less easily integratable than the two data bases from which they are drawn. The integration of knowledge and insight must be at the data base level, must be God-centered in terms of Christ's role in nature and grace, and must be pragmatic. The integration effort must be designed to comprehend holistically the total universe. Comprehensive and pragmatic integration means acknowledging that the universe in all its aspects manifests God's nature and is teleological. God's nature is so complex that it manifests itself paradoxically in his world: in unity and diversity, development and stasis, and freedom and determinism.

Berry has illumined the theological perspective with which science can be done but must rethink his notion of paradox as a useful source of categories. Some of what he calls paradoxes are not. The polarity between the literal and metaphoric, between the individual and group, and between the one and the many constitutes tension but not paradox. Berry's suggestion is designed to clear some philosophical ground. The idea needs further, more vigorous exploration.

Truth from Science

Theology and psychology are both sciences in their own right, stand legitimately on their own foundations, and read carefully are two books of God's revelation. They are not alien in any inherent sense. When they seem paradoxical or disparate, it must always be because of disfunction on one of three counts. Either the professional has failed to read the Bible well enough or to investigate the sciences of the natural world thoroughly enough, or has distorted the science of the theological or natural world by arbitrary dogmatism, not properly constrained by sound investigation of God's word in creation or Scripture, or has drawn erroneous conclusions in either of those investigations.

Wherever truth is disclosed it is always God's truth. Whether it is found in general revelation or special revelation, it is truth which has equal warrant with all other truth. Some truth may have greater weight than other truth in a specific situation, but there is no difference in its warrant as *truth*.

Koteskey begins to understand that fact. Carter gives at least lip service to it. Don Tweedie denies it. In contesting a paper read some years ago in Atlanta entitled "Psychological Theory and Christian Experience in Psychotherapy," Dr. Tweedie made an impassioned claim that because Carl Rogers had left his evangelical moorings years ago his contribution to scholarship was not shaped and infused by the Holy Spirit, and therefore his insights regarding psychological dynamics and therapy could be of no value or usefulness to the Christian scientist or practitioner. Apparently, for Tweedie the Christian and secularist do not differ merely in philosophical perspective nor in ways of integrating their scientific insights into their world views. They differ in that the scientific endeavor of each in theology and psychology amount to their practicing different kinds of science. Dr. Tweedie apparently does not know about general revelation and its relevance, or about God's common grace.

Even worse is Jay E. Adams, who apparently never even thought of the notion that all truth as God's truth, has equal warrant, whether truth from nature or Scripture. He absorbs all psychology into his theology. The tragedy is compounded, moreover, because his theology is not rooted in God's unconditional grace but in a conditional works-righteousness.

The integration model will be a dead end for the dialogic quest unless the problems are solved regarding the alienness of psychology and theology, and the absorption of one in the other. To solve them will require the discarding of both the term *integration* and the conceptual model it implies.

The real issue in the quest for Christian responsibility in the helping professions is the search for a method and model of employing theology from a psychological perspective and psychology from a theological perspective. That perspectival model of theoretical and applied professional work, allows for taking seriously the legitimacy of both sciences and acknowledging in operational models that both sciences are generically one and not mutually alien. The *perspectival model* assumes the universal lordship of Christ and God's sovereignty in all things.

Two Principles

There are two principles that must be taken seriously in laying the ground work for the perspectival model. The first regards what constitutes the distinctiveness of being Christian in the helping professions. In the realm of psychological theory development, the first principle of being Christian is not that our scientific achievement supports, reinforces, or coordinates with our theology or faith, but that it reflects God's truth from his created world in our science. To be distinctively Christian requires that psychological theory development produce warrantable scientific theory. In the realm of psychological practice, the first principle of being Christian is, not that it conforms to our theology, but that it is the most superbly sound psychotherapy possible. To be a Christian therapist requires first of all that I be a thoroughly effective therapist. Otherwise one may be both a Christian of sorts and a therapist of sorts but not yet a Christian therapist.

Sound psychological theory and practice genuinely enhances the patient's progress from pathology to full-orbed personhood. God designed what that is. Christians perceive it in varying degrees. Full-orbed personhood may be achieved by patients to varying levels of completeness or functionality. Sound psychology, which brings the patient, for example, out of depression to emotional resilience and stability, is just as Christian at that level as at the level affording the final stages of maturity: spiritual certainty and peace as the person in Christ. Even if that deliverance from depression is done by a secularist, it is a Kingdom act and a Christian enterprise, though it may never achieve the completeness it could under a comparably effective Christian therapist.

What makes practice in the helping professions Christian is less the imparting of biblical information or religious practices to the patient, and more the enhancement of healthy functionality of the human as person: in the direction of completeness in body, mind, and spirit. That practice of the helping professions that is preoccupied with the final step of wholeness, spiritual maturity, will usually short-circuit the therapeutic process and put the religious dynamic of the patient or therapist straight into the typical religious patient's psychopathology. Such practice tends to reinforce, for example, such sickness as neurotic guilt, depression from constipated anger and low self-esteem, compulsivity, and the psychotic decision of the schizophrenic to exchange the real world for a fantasy world.

The *second principle* regarding being Christian in the helping professions is the necessity of the incarnational style of the professional in those roles. As in all forms of incarnation, that of Jesus Christ supremely so, the import and impact of the role is more direct and life shaping for the incarnating one than for the object of that person's ministry or service.

The Christian therapist fills the role of incarnating for the patient healing expectations, direction, and certification from a Christian perspective. The requirements of incarnating the healing power and technique directly shape the therapist: conditioning the therapist's values, attitudes, goals, insights, techniques, and passions in terms of the divine claims of sound faith and sound science. The impact upon the client is indirect. Being a Christian psychologist has more to do with what is happening in the therapist's attitude, thought, experience, and professional and personal quality than it has to with what happens to the patient. The impact upon the patient should manifest itself in the way the Christian therapist's perspective and nature seep through the work into the patient's experience of the therapist's quality as a person and professional. The therapist's patient-handling technique and expectations regarding what health means must incarnate sound Christianity and sound science. Perhaps ultimately the impact desired is that of the therapist's world view seeping into the patient's experience.

Eight Possibilities

The eight possibilities for shaping the therapist's development for the incarnational role as a Christian in the helping professions are eight biblical themes. The themes ought to be incorporated into the Christian professional's conceptualization of life and the work. The themes are the biblical concepts of personhood, alienation, grace, sin, discipline, "the wounded healer," mortality, and celebration as a way of life. The biblical concepts ring true to and illumine psychological theory and practice at key points. God's anthropology illumines sound psychosocial research.

The biblical theology of human personhood is surprising and profound. Unconditional grace theology is clearly the central biblical theme from the text tradition of the Yahwist in the Pentateuch through the nonimprecatory psalms, to the covenant theology in the prophets, especially Second Isaiah, Hosea, Zechariah, and Malachi, and into the Gospel tradition of how Jesus handled people. In that whole literary fabric, one thing is overwhelmingly clear. Human persons are unconditionally cherished by God, in spite of themselves. God so loved the world that he created it. He made humans inherently imagers of himself. God invested all persons with an unnegotiable and inviolable dignity, from the outset imputing to each the status of compatriot of God. The Eden story does not speak of humanity as children, servants, or subordinates of God but as divine compatriots. God visited Adam and Eve in the cool of the evening, and they shared God's enterprises of keeping the garden and naming the animals. Adam was placed in a complimentary relationship with God.

That imputed status was never abbrogated, despite Adam's declaration of independence, under the threat of death. God's response to the Fall was to change the ground rules at God's expense and reaffirm humankind's dignified status and destiny. In that inviolable status every human person has only two potential conditions: to be in a posture that rings true to that God-given status and therefore true to self, or to be inauthentic in perspective, disposition, or behavior and suffer the dissonance and dis-ease inherent to that inauthenticity.

Through it all, God remains preoccupied with human need not human naughtiness, with human failure of destiny more than of duty, and with the redeemd potential not with the sinful past. If God confirms patients and therapists in that quality of personhood, Christian psychological theory and practice must be based upon it. Patients are free to be what they are for the sake of what they can become, before the face of God.

The biblical theology of alienation starts with the story of the Fall. It describes the human person as a child who has lost touch with the Father's hand. The state of fallenness is expressed in Augustine's pathetic prayer, "Thou has made us for thyself, and our souls are restless until they rest, O God, in thee."

The fallenness of humanity is obvious. Its psychological

consequences are evident every day everywhere. The brokenness and disjointedness of the psyche of all humans is empirical expression of the human longing for our Father's hand, the primal anxiety permeating everything, and the thirst for life as anxiety reduction. The many compensatory strategies incited by all that are frequently additional dynamics that produce pathology. Religion, particularly the Judeo-Christian religion of divine grace, is a significant anxiety-reduction mechanism. The uniqueness of the Judeo-Christian theology of grace is that it reveals God as unconditionally gracious, while all other religion represents him as a threat. Moreover, the anxiety-reduction factor in all other religions is legalistic self-justification. It is the strategy of forcing God's favor through the performance of liturgical or ethical requirements, devised by religionists, for measuring up to God's standards. In the Judeo-Christian religion the anxiety-reduction mechanism is exclusively that of grace, "unconditional positive regard" for the sinner. That anxiety reduction is reinforced, of course, by the opportunity for the life of gratitude that can follow so great a salvation. So the theology of alienation is critical to the Christian professional's perception of self and others and the recognition of God's way of dealing with that as the Christian's analogue for handling people.

The biblical theology of grace, therefore, is critically informative of any sound psychological or psychotherapeutic concept or strategy. In the Bible, grace is unconditional, arbitrary, universal, exploitable, and radical. It is unconditional as in the parable of the prodigal son, universal as in the Genesis 12 and 17 covenant for the healing of the nations, and it is radical in that it cuts through to the center of human alienation, whether humans like it or not. Moreover, God's grace perpetually reaffirms the compatriot status of all humans with God, in spite of themselves. That has been a difficult perception for the believing community to hold to throughout history. The Jews took about a thousand years to loose it, the Christians five hundred, and the Reformers about two hundred. Humans have a native compulsive proclivity to try to get their own hands on the controls of justification, because accepting free grace is so scary and so nearly unbelievable for people who perceive themselves as "not OK children." The Christian's model of pathology and patient care needs to be formed and informed by the radical realities of this biblical theme.

The biblical theology of sin is likewise crucial to the perspectival model of Christian professionalism. Sin, contrary to popular opinion, is a failure in achievement of authenticity to self and of full-orbed personhood in Christ. It is a distortion and distraction to lesser achievements. It cannot be compensated for. It can only be converted from. Metanoia is the only solution. That is possible only to the person who has heard the announcement that he is forgiven and accepted unconditionally. Nietzsche said the courage to be, in this hopelessly tragic world, is the ability to stand at the brink of the abyss of nothingness and hear without flinching the announcement that God is dead. The real story that he could have known is that the courage to be, in this fractured and alienated world, is the ability to stand in the middle of the hopelessness of human alienation and hear the announcement that God has embraced us in spite of ourselves and realize that if God is for us no one can be against us. Ultimately, each person cannot even be against himself or herself as an obstruction to divine grace and acceptance. Such a perception comes from hearing the word that human destiny is to realize in full-orbed personhood the palpable experiences of the regal status of compatriot, which God has imputed to humans in spite of themselves. God never abrogates that status. He simply waits for us to achieve the self-actualization that expresses it. Sin is falling short of that expectation.

God's law is not a threat, implying a conditional

relationship, infraction bringing loss of favor. It is rather a constitution for the kingdom of shalom: peace and prosperity in all facets of life. It is interesting in this regard that Jesus was preoccupied, as were the prophets, with social psychological wholeness, not practices of private piety and personal purity. Such preoccupation is idolatry, manufacturing out of self a plastic doll, as opposed to celebrating the compatriot status grace establishes. Sin is bondage and pathology, because it is a distraction to a distorted destiny, a constrained striving, compared with maturity in God's grace which is the glorious freedom of the children of God. Thus Luther could say, "Sin boldly," and mean it. "Since you are going to be a sinner today, step out boldly into today, living in the assurance of God's grace!"

The biblical theology of discipline is the theme of discipleship. Getting well or doing good is enacting grace. Discipline is the endeavor of beginning down the road of forgiveness of self and others, of acceptance of self and others, of unconditionally caring for self and others, and of reflecting the divine analogue. Discipleship is a troth with self and God to incarnate that divine grace-dynamic that infuses the universe. It is the troth "to forsake all other foci and keep thee only to the Kingdom destiny." Jesus urged people to such discipline by the grace with which he handled them. The adulterous woman he urged, "I do not condemn you. Go and do not do it anymore. It is untrue to yourself." To the Samaritan woman he gave the insight that spirituality, not religiousity, is the issue. Peter, the denier, Christ ordained to build the church, and Matthew reports that in the garden Jesus grabbed Judas and said, *"Friend,* how did it come to this?" Biblical discipleship means being bound to Christ, to be free in grace. It means to live eschatologically: before the face of God. Since that is what life is designed to be, Christian expectations for therapists and Christian possibilities for clients will be shaped by such discipleship.

Henri Nouwen has the finest word on the *biblical theological theme of the wounded healer.* He takes the suffering servant notion of the Old Testament, which is also epitomized in the messianic theology of the New Testament, and points out that there are four doors for God, and the Christian, into the heart of humanity: the door of the woundedness of the world, the woundedness of any given generation, the woundedness of the individual, and the woundedness of the healer. He points out that this wounded healer theme implies that all grace, growth, and healing are communicated or incited by starting where the healer and the person to be healed are. The humanness and brokenness of both must be affirmed. The healer's role is not to remove the pain of life but to interpret it. Moreover, the evidence in the healer of woundedness and pain and of the transcendence or constructive endurance of it helps to heal the patient. Carl Jung's notion of the archetype healer projected by the patient upon the therapist and the value of the healer sharing his or her own growth dynamics in therapy are relevant here. The wounded healer can become the model and the incarnation of risk taking in growth and healing.

The biblical theological theme of mortality is directly related to the idea of the wounded healer. The Bible gives little impetus to the perfectionist notions that building the Kingdom will bring the elimination of the mortality and brokenness of the world. The Bible, instead, affirms our mortality and the world's brokenness and emphasizes the strategies for making godly sense in that setting. That, after all, is what grace is all about. The brokenness, humanness, and pathology is affirmed—and that we are dying men and women in a generation of dying men and women. It acknowledges both the magnificence and malignancy in the universe. The persistent malignancy is pathologically denied in our cultural idealization of the bigger and better. The Bible says it's OK to vary from the idealized norm. It is acceptable to age, wrinkle, decrease, distort, weaken, become more dependent, and even die. In fact, to die can be a real gain, according to St. Paul. Youthfulness is not the focus of meaning in the biblical concept of mortality, but maturation is. Patients need to feel in therapists the Christian realization that it is a supportable, and perhaps even a celebratable, condition to be a human, mortal, dying person, before the face of God.

The finest biblical illumination of what it means behaviorally to be Christian in our work and world is the theme of *celebration.* It is a revealing clinical and biblical fact that people who can be grateful can be healthy and people who are incapable of generating spontaneous and authentic gratitude are unable to be healthy. They do not have the interior machinery or dynamics for it. The German Reformers knew that four hundred years ago and wrote it into that warm, human document the Heidelberg Catechism, with its focus upon gratitude as the Christian's way of life. Celebration as gratitude may take the form of worship, or the childlike posture before our Father that we call prayer. Celebration may be exhilarated joy for the providence of God in life. To be Christian means to be like children celebrating the Father's beneficence. A Christian therapist who sees life as that kind of enterprise will incarnate for the patient crucial elements of celebration, in the clinical spirit and process.

Twelve Practical Applications

The *twelve practical applications* of biblical theology to the psychotherapeutic setting can be detailed briefly.

1. Recognition of the biblical themes leads to the assumption of a preestablished identity for the patient. It is the identity of one whom God affirms as compatriot. That identity needs to be recovered or enhanced in the therapy. Though that may never be explained in the therapy, it will

shape the therapist's affirmation of the patient and hence the patient's experience of being affirmed by the therapist. The therapist is in that sense a priest of God for that needy person.

2. The biblical themes imply for the patient a certified and secure destiny, infused with clear purpose for self-realization in the Kingdom context.

3. They insure for the patient the experience of acceptance in keeping with the analogue of God's unconditional grace for the patient and the therapist. The biblical themes introduce into the therapeutic milieu a dynamic that can work toward the defusing of neurotic guilt, unproductive remorse, hopelessness, unresolved grief, self-pity, compulsivity, and some of the need for schizoid ideation. That Christian perspective also potentially decreases the need for the defeating processes of masking, denial, self-justification, self-affliction, and the conversion reactions so often produced by these. Moreover, the insight afforded by the biblical themes frees one for informed and constructive self-acceptance.

4. The perspective the themes give the therapist, and potentially the patient, provides the foundation for a life-style of dignity—not a life-style of self-abnegation and demeanment, but of being cherished and affirmed.

5. The biblical perspective can take the panic out of therapy for the therapist. Since God is God and grace is grace, even when we are not experiencing it, the therapist need not feel as though the weight of the world is on him or her and as though the therapist's own personhood or destiny hangs on the outcome of "this case."

6. These themes afford the relief, affirmed self-esteem, and certification as a person that are likely to take the form of a sense of worthiness imputed to and inherent in the patient as person, rather than worthiness earned and dependent upon the patient's behavior.

7. These biblical perspectives can reduce the need for

anxiety in the therapist and decrease the therapist-pathology with which the patient has to deal.

8. They provide a broad base of insight and perspective for building wholesome transference and countertransference.

9. They afford a coherent context for all of life, healthy or pathological. That context is God's disposition of inviolable goodwill, not divine threat.

10. They expand the potential for risk taking toward growth and integrated maturity, by means of their predominant function of constructive anxiety reduction. The entire mode of these themes is freedom. They afford relief from constraints that distract from the patient's Christian self-actualization.

11. The biblical perspective frees the therapist to be human without being care-less; to play God as necessary in therapeutic decision-making and method without losing sight of his real stature and role; and to exercise a sound sense of humor about himself, about God, the patient, and pathology, and the fragile enterprise of therapy.

12. The biblical perspective releases persons to die well. That relief attacks the ultimate panic that stands as a specter behind all pathology.

Conclusion

Theology and faith are cognitive-emotive processes. Therefore, their function for ill or good must be most relevant and applicable to disorders that are cognitive or emotive in source. That means that healthy dynamics and perspectives in theology and faith will affect the potential health of the therapist and patient in such psychosocial disorders. Religious dynamics may be somewhat less relevant in psychopathology that has a body-chemistry source, though even then, healthy theology and faith may be invaluable in management of the symptoms.

However, with the increasing evidence for the two-way switching function of the hypothalamus in channeling or controlling the impact of endocrine disorders upon the psychological field and of psychic disorders on the endocrine function, the role of healthy or pathological theology, faith, or spirituality becomes increasingly interesting with regard to the role in, or impact upon, even those psychopathologies that appear to root in distortions of body chemistry.

Therefore, concerns about theological perspective, faith commitment, religious experience, and spiritual maturity are becoming increasingly vital therapeutic issues. The concern to be a Christian professional really is a crucial one.

The following chapters endeavor to explore the issues raised in this introductory chapter and to access them at the depth they deserve.

CHAPTER *1*

Anxiety and the
Rise of Religious Experience

Human religion is universal. Religious experience and expression is evidenced by and significantly shapes all culture. Apparently to be religious is native to being human.

Humans everywhere worship. To do so seems innate in the personality. Liturgies of worship grow out of psychological and spiritual sources deep within the human personality. Those psychic (psyche) sources of religion are closely related to the native human anxiety patterns discernible in personality. Some forms of worship and religion meet the deep human psychic needs better than other forms. Most religious practices in life and history reinforce the anxiety of man through the frustrating dynamics of guilt and the sense of the ultimate helplessness in the face of morality problems and mortality threat. Authentic Judeo-Christianity is unique in its gospel of grace. That cuts to the center of the human problem with the assurance of both the meaning of life and the promise of immortality. Distinguishing between what is authentic spirituality and what is psychic pathology is, therefore, crucial.

The original version of this article appeared in *The Journal of Psychology and Theology* 3 (Winter 1975) and appears here by permission.

37

Already in the antique world of Greece and Rome, it was strongly suggested that all men need to worship. Despite the Renaissance, modern thought has consistently suspected that ancient suggestion to be true. Since Sir James George Frazer's notable work, *The Golden Bough,* was first published in 1890, the Western world has scientifically affirmed that humanness and religiosity always and everywhere appear together. The Eastern world has known the certainty of that fact for a number of millennia.

The only remaining potential challenge to this axiom about religion and humanness lies with the paleontologists like Richard Leakey who presume to uncover the character and culture of the original hominids and hominoids. It now appears that they will make good on their presumption. If so, they may turn up a prereligious hominid. However, the current evidence is against it, since among the earliest tools of all anthropoids so far identified, have been included ritual and funerary utensils of an apparently religious nature. If Leakey looks one day into the sunken sockets of a prereligious hominid skull, of course, there will still remain the problem of definition of terms. How will he certify that the primitive character who lost his godless head so long ago was really prereligious in theological tendencies as well as in tools? How, moreover, will it be decided which hominoid is hominid and which hominid is Homo sapiens?

Humanness as we know it, in any case, is apparently essentially religious. Scholars in the field of comparative religion have unveiled a wealth of information in the last hundred years concerning the nature and meaning of the religious character of humanness. In so doing, they have demonstrated the significant religious role of symbol in ritual and theology. Out of recognition of the universal religious role of symbols and symbol making arose the awareness of intricate interrelationship between religion and human psychology—between the life of the spirit and the life of the psyche (Jung, 1964).

In the last two decades vigorous and productive work has been done in the psychology of religion. The enterprise has depended heavily upon the pioneering work of William James and his *Varieties of Religious Experience.* That in turn was anticipated in theology by the epistemological quest of Immanuel Kant and by the entire fabric of the theology of Schleiermacher. It was Schleiermacher, after all, who defined the common ground from which all religious experience grows up. He built his Christian theology upon the fact that the feeling of dependence is the universal and constant character of human consciousness that makes man necessarily religious. Carl Jung (1958) produced a major step forward in relating the world of the spirit and the world of the psyche with his description of human anxiety as the form in which man realizes the "experience of dependence." Seward Hiltner (1963) carried the idea from anxiety to the relief of grace.[1]

Human religious experience and expression, it is therefore urged, rises from the native and universal human experience of anxiety. Arapura, in his superb little book, *Religion as Anxiety and Tranquility,* refers to the "non-accidental but necessary character of religion" (p. 7). He illumines the matter greatly by pointing out that the essential or necessary character of human religiosity is a product of human self-consciousness, "which like *being* is what *necessarily is.*" He goes on to argue that as humanness implies self-consciousness, self-consciousness implies anxiety, and anxiety is in interplay with the vital urges of the human organism toward achieving tranquility.

Karen Horney illumines this point with her useful definition of anxiety. After describing the kinship of anxiety with fear, she goes on to point out that,

> When a mother is afraid that her child will die when it has only a pimple or a slight cold we speak of anxiety; but if she is afraid when the child has a serious illness we call her reaction fear. If someone is afraid whenever he stands on a height or when he has to discuss a topic he knows well, we call his reaction anxiety; if someone is afraid when he loses his way high up in the mountains during a heavy thunderstorm we would speak of fear. Thus far we should have a simple and neat distinction: fear is a reaction that is proportionate to the danger one has to face, whereas anxiety is a disproportionate reaction to danger, or even a reaction to imaginary danger.[2]

Horney's contention here is similar to Freud's distinction between objective and neurotic anxiety. Freud called the former an intelligible reaction to danger and the latter an irrational or exaggerated one. Horney is dissatisfied, however, to allow her simple definition to stand untouched. It has one flaw in her judgment. It does not distinguish between what is proportionate in one culture from what is disproportionate in another. Anxiety about taboos may be appropriate in the value setting of a primitive culture. Anxiety about the same thing in twentieth century American culture would be disproportionate and neurotic. Horney, therefore, helpfully amplifies her definition as follows:

> All these considerations suggest a change in the definition. Fear and anxiety are both proportionate reactions to danger, but in the case of fear the danger is a transparent, objective one and in the case of anxiety it is hidden and subjective. That is, the intensity of the anxiety is proportionate to the meaning the situation has for the person concerned, and the reasons why he is thus anxious are essentially unknown to him.
>
> The practical implication of the distinction between fear and anxiety is that the attempt to argue a neurotic out of his anxiety—the method of persuasion—is useless. His anxiety concerns not the situation as it stands actually in reality, but the situation as it appears to him.[3]

The perception to which Horney refers at this juncture is often a subconscious perception of an anxiety-affording situation. Humans often have anxiety, therefore, without being clearly aware of it. Nonetheless, that anxiety calls for resolution. The native forces of the human physical and psychic organism that press for tranquility function as vigorously on the subconscious as on the conscious level. "In fact, we seem to go to any lengths to escape anxiety or to avoid feeling it" (p. 46).

The fact that anxiety, whether disproportionate or proportionate, conscious or subconscious, is frequently irrational and manifests itself in irrational pressures toward resolution, does not discount the problem but rather complicates it. Irrational anxiety or expression of anxiety "presents an implicit admonition that something within us is out of gear, and therefore, it is a challenge to overhaul something within us."[4] The human organism employs four strategies to effect that change. Humans rationalize, deny, or narcotize anxiety, or "avoid thoughts, feeling impulses and situations which might arouse it."[5] In the character and potential creativity of these forms of anxiety management lies the human religious potential.

Albert C. Outler assessed this precisely and positively when he wrote,

Religious anxiety is both neurotic and ontological at one and the same time. It is neurotic to the extent that it misconstrues the symbols of "groundlessness" and so reacts *in*appropriately. From this follows the kaleidoscope of religiosity—with its superstitions and stultifying effects that the psychiatrist knows all too well. At the same time, our sense of alienation from God turns into a dread of God's alienation from us. The Deity is, quite literally, dreadful, and the guilt-ridden soul is anxious lest the offended Creator will jerk the rug out from under the offending creature, leaving him suspended over nothing! Augustine speaks of his dread of *abyssus*. The literal meaning of this term is "ocean-depths." Augustine had an anxiety-affect about the ocean: It reminded him—as neurotic anxiety feelings may remind anyone—of life's unsteadiness. Neurotic or no, the symbols of disequilibrium are reminders of the profoundest threat we ever recognize—life's lapsing into meaninglessness.

> . . . Anxiety is the inner dread of this unsteady support. Yet the truth is that there is no such thing as a firm footing in the created world itself. Those creaturely values on which we depend do not pretend to be a firm and final ground. Our feeling of groundlessness (and the dread of it) is meant to prod us toward the truth—that God alone is our true Ground and End.[6]

Out of this physico-psychological ferment between anxiety and tranquility come forth human religious experience and expression. Religion is part of the machinery for mediation between the forces of death and life in the inner man.

How and why anxiety is born in man and gives rise to religion is, of course, a further question. Another matter still, is the question of the efficiency with which religions of various kinds succeed in managing or responding to the native human angst. In observing the religious quest of the ancient Egyptians, Barbara Mertz signified the commonality of their predicament with ours four millennia later. She described the native need and genius for religion in her closing paragraphs like this:

> Whether they feared their demons or not, the Egyptians did fear death—the first physical death and that second death from which there is no resurrection. They spent a good part of their lives fighting annihilation, and in so doing they built up the most complicated structure of mortuary ritual any people ever produced. We are the beneficiaries of it, in terms of museum collections and scholarly books; and perhaps we will not find the painted mummy cases and weird amulets so bizarre if we see beneath their extravagance, a common human terror and a common hope.[7]

That common human terror and the common hope is the springboard of all religion (Horney). The Egyptian system may not have been as effective or as true as contemporary Christianity, but the crucial point here is that both spring from the same native humanness, and endeavor to meet the same need.

What then is that need? It seems apparent that all humans wrestle with four basic questions regarding the meaning of things. The questions concern origins, nature and destiny, the "oughts" of life, and aesthetics. To be human seems invariably to mean that we have a thirst to know where things came from, where things are going, what we ought, therefore, to do (ethics), and how we ought to carry ourselves (style). In addition the native human need to know what is the good, true, and beautiful makes everyone in some degree an aesthete.

All these major questions represent, and together they comprehend, that massive world of the unknown into which the lately womb-harbored infant comes bumping and splashing down the birth canal. From the moment of birth, obviously, humans begin the long, psychologically arduous adventure of accommodation to the massive, mostly uncontrollable, and therefore threatening unknown of life in this world. Nearly as soon as the newly self-conscious child achieves some measure of control, stability, and security in his ever-expanding new world, he is imposed upon by a newer and even more unmanageable unknown: death. He finds that the arduous and threatening adventure is mostly and ultimately a tragic adventure. Born of this anxiety, then, is the perpetual human tension of mind and spirit between the paradise of tranquility he can envision and the possibilities of terror he really experiences. The "once and future paradise" becomes a permanent part of his psychic symbolism and character. Obviously, for humans it is a relatively short step from such symbolics to the fashioning of God or gods "after one's own anxious image" of the way things are.

The question should be raised, however, why humans need to deal so gravely and seriously with the four major meaning questions in life. Why is it not possible for humans, as Harry Golden counseled in his book, simply to relax and *Enjoy, Enjoy*? The answer, I judge, is the persistent presence of the problem of evil.

It is a fact of life that all of us begin, nearly as soon as we become self-conscious, to discern that we are all capable, at one and the same time, of being majestically magnificent and of being miserably malicious. We learn early, I believe, that there is in the universe itself a comparable potential for magnificence and malignancy. In the face of that and the anxiety it reinforces in us, we are driven to the pursuit of meaning. Likely there is something of the divine image in that insatiable quest.

It was this impasse regarding the incongruity of evil, finally, that shaped Kierkegaard's definition of angst and religion.[8] Rudolf Otto looked for the definitive stuff of religion in *das numinöse Gefühl,* a kind of mystical or intuitive level of self-consciousness in the presence of the human predicament, which would afford revelation of the certainty and character of God's existence. Eliade seems to be closer to the realities of experience and fact when he asserts that the human quest for meaning arises out of the "terror of history."

> How shall we resolve the paradoxical situation created by the two-fold fact that man, on the one hand, finds himself in *time,* given over to history, and on the other he knows that he will be "damned" if he allows himself to be exhausted by temporality and historicity; that consequently, he must at all costs find *in this world* a road that issues upon a transhistorical and atemporal plane.[9]

"Our common human terror," Eliade argues, is our anxious awareness of the terminal character of finitude. Tillich observed that "finitude in awareness is anxiety." Our "common hope" is the "paradise" that comes with transcending finitude, which paradise we can envision but hardly create. To achieve meaning, namely, "the certainty that historical tragedies have a transhistorical meaning," is to achieve freedom from finitude and anxiety, declares Eliade.[10] That achievement is the business of religion.

Arapura summarizes the entire discussion in one essential statement. "The sense of the wrongness of existence is common . . . to all of mankind's consciousness."[11] This sense of "wrongness apparently focuses for mankind especially in anxiety about our mortality and our morality."[12] Religious experience and expression is the dynamic process of attempting to structure a response to the facts that we are dying, dealing with (mortality) the unknown of death, and we are, therefore, inadequate, dealing with (morality) the loss of worthwhileness.[13] The religious dimension of humans is the psychological machinery and ritual tools produced by the human organism to manage security. Religion is the process of reducing the profound anxiety about the deadliness of life to the profound tranquility of salvation: eternal life.

In this reduction process, as suggested above, it is a relatively short step from anxiety, the sense of wrongness, internalized as personal guilt, to the projection upon the human universe of a concept of a threatening God. As children do, so do all humans internalize threat and pain as guilt. If we are guilty, we are guilty before the face of someone who stands in a position of power or at least authority. So, from the threat of the unknown within and without, humans move to anxiety, hence to guilt and a sense of the wrongness of things, and from guilt to a projection called God.

The seriousness of this dynamic is not changed by Neitzsche's point that the "bad conscience" often produces much creative energy and productivity. Nietzsche declared, "The bad conscience is a sickness but it is a sickness as pregnancy is one."[14]

The seriousness of the dynamic religious process from anxiety, to guilt, to God is unmitigated by that because it usually produces an ultimate psychological and theological impasse, rather than a resolution of anxiety (Jung, 1938). Taking the whole of the history of human religion into view, it is immediately apparent that normally what one compulsively is driven to undertake in religious quest one does not have the ability to achieve, namely, transcendence above finitude, morality, mortality, and the divine threat.

In consequence, what man usually achieves in his reach from anxiety, to guilt, to God is a god fashioned in man's own "threat image." That god then reigns as superego, imposing confinement not freedom, reinforcing anxiety not relief, producing legalistic rituals for the liturgies of worship and the liturgies of life (ethics and morality). The only alternative in the history of religions has been the Judeo-Christian concept of grace: God who arbitrarily transcends the "wrongness of the universe" and man and unconditionally accepts man as he is, assuring him of the relief of worthwhileness and immortality.

This is the reason that, despite the prevalent popular notion to the contrary, there are two, and only two, kinds of religion in the history of man: those which operate on the assumption that God is for us and those which operate on the assumption that God is against us. The latter build intricate strategies in ethics and worship to provide techniques for self-justification. The former express themselves in authentic celebration of grace and gratitude. The latter is the psychological bondage of a blind alley. The former is the freedom of life as an open-ended, creative quest in which every risk—theological, moral, and spiritual—is ultimately safe; for "grace is greater than all our sins."

In this regard a number of observations are crucial. First, in all the history of human religion, the religion of grace appeared only once: in the Judeo-Christian experience. It sprang forth in Abraham's vision in Genesis 12 and 17 and is epitomized in the way Jesus of Nazareth handled people. Second, all other religious forms in history have assumed a threatening god and are self-justification strategies for anxious humans. Incidentally, Buddhism and Hinduism, which are so often compared with Christianity, are in point of fact escapist programs designed to enact a pattern of psychological denial of divine threat and the pain of the human enigma. That pattern is the practice of karma to achieve Nirvana. Third, by the time of Christ, Judaism had long since lost its clean vision of grace and had become a full-blown paganism in that it conceived of God as a threatening deity to be propitiated by legalistic rituals. Likewise, by the fifth century after Christ, Christianity had lost its clean vision of the radical and unconditional character of grace personified in Christ and so evident in the *pericope de adultera* of John 8, and had fallen into the crass legalistic paganism of a religion of human self-justification. Luther cut through the "God-threat" religion to a position of radical trust in unconditional character of grace. However, it took Reformation Christianity less than two centuries to return to legalistic theological and ethical strategies designed as tools for man to manipulate a threatening God into kindness he would otherwise have spurned.

Consequently, in the total history of religion, historical Judeo-Christianity as well as all others, the psychological pathologies of massive anxiety must be taken as seriously as any more ethereal or less human etiological factors. In evaluating Christian or Judaic ritual, biblical or extra-biblical, truth depends upon an adequate appreciation of the role of motivating anxiety before judgments are made regarding the role of supernatural revelation. Only then can one separate the human cultural and psychological garbage from the clear good news of grace. For example, Judeo-Christian prayer or ritual which is designed to motivate God to do something benevolent which he would not have good enough sense to do if left alone is one thing. Prayer and worship as celebration of gratitude for grace is a profoundly different thing. The difference is between the pagan product of human anxiety and the profound Pauline perception that God is for us, not against us (Rom. 8).

The sole recommendation for the Judeo-Christian grace insight as truth, moreover, is the fact that Abraham's insight and Jesus' behavior are the only solution to man's native psychic predicament of overwhelming anxiety regarding the "wrongness of existence" and the silence of the "great Absent One." Jesus is there in history. His way of handling people affirms our worthwhileness and resolves anxiety into tranquility by the psychological dynamics of cherishing acceptance. He affirms us as we are, affording thereby the psychic freedom to become what we are potentially in body, mind, and psyche. That is man's only chance—humanity being what it is.

This leads to two concluding points. First, much of what goes for Judaic or Christian religion is psychological distortion or full-blown pathology. Pastors and professional counselors must be willing and able to differentiate severely between the two. Moreover, much of what goes for theological and ethical truth is, the consequence, not of the insight of grace, but of the pathology of the psyche. Authentic evaluation of the current patterns of the charismatic movements, for example, cannot be carried out effectively without an awareness of the possibility that they are no more than a repetition in a mystical escapist frame of the long-familiar super-achievement designs of much of pagan conservative Christianity.

What religious forms are anxiety-produced strategies for self-certification and inevitably self-defeating designs for security? Legalistic or compulsive frenzy is only another alternative to grace, a manifestation of psychic pathology, and potentially unproductive psychological processes of sublimation and denial, which ultimately stultify the achievement of true wholeness and personhood.

Finally, it is obvious that the human anxiety syndrome does not adequately account for the unique and crucial faith insight of Judeo-Christianity. However, equally significant for Christians in the counseling and helping professions is the realization that the human need addressed by the unique grace insight is as much the product of the human anxiety syndrome as the characteristic religious nature of any human in any religious tradition. It is as though we were all created to celebrate the security of living life, as it were "hand in hand" with God as Father, whereas we are cast by our sense of alienation into the predicament of having lost the touch of his hand. That may just be what the terror of history really amounts to. That may be the real dimension of our mystification and "confusion of face." The ancient Hebrew myth of a garden tragedy may be closer to truth than is history. Our common human terror and our common hope may well be as St. Augustine urged. "Thou hast made us for thyself, and our souls are restless until they rest, O God, in thee."

In any case, as those skilled to deal with psychic pathology, it is crucial that we keep clearly in focus the psychic source of human religion in the universal phenomenon of profound anxiety about our very being and existence. That perspective is crucial to an intelligible discrimination and evaluation of the high incidence of religious complexities and fixations in neurotic and psychotic pathologies. Moreover, there is a high likelihood of direct relationship between anxiety as the source of religion, on the one hand, and the typical sex-religion disorder syndrome in mental illness on the other. Sex, after all, is the second most anxiety-inducing phenomenon in man's life, only after religion. Furthermore, sexuality and spirituality, if traced back to their central sources in the root of man's being, are likely the same phenomenon, the same dynamic force.

In any case, it is crucial that authentic religious experience and psychic pathology or its consequence be differentiated. Then worship can be real and redemptively healing. Then spirituality can be freedom, not bondage. Then life can be the relief of grace.

CHAPTER 2

The Biblical
Theological Underpinnings

Introduction

In his admirable book, *The Yahwist: The Bible's First Theologian,* Peter Ellis demonstrated satisfactorily that the undergirding stratum of Judeo-Christian biblical theology is the sturdy tradition of unconditional and universal divine grace.[1] Ellis' argument assumes the accuracy of the general claims of the *Formegeschicte Schule* of biblical criticism and its notions regarding multiple, distinct, and, to some degree, disparate pentateuchal source traditions. With a trained analytic eye one can trace readily and with considerable precision the theological strains of the Yahwist and Priestly traditions and, to a somewhat lesser extent, an Elohist theological tradition throughout the rest of the Hebrew Bible. Furthermore, the great theologians of the New Testament had little difficulty demonstrating that the life and ministry of Jesus Christ incarnated precisely the thrust of the Yahwist theologian. The Christian Scriptures, in consequence, became a towering theological and pastoral expression of the applied contours of God's radical grace.

Brevard S. Childs has done the world of biblical study a fine favor with his recent book *Introduction to the Old Testament as Scripture.*[2] Professor Childs argues for a decreasing emphasis upon *Formegeschichte* principles of pentateuchal source traditions and an increasing emphasis upon the editorial redaction that the scriptures experienced, as the believing community in Judaism and early Christendom employed those scriptures as authoritative canonical revelation. Childs' book will undoubtedly constitute a new watershed of biblical scholarship. However, though Childs finds the tension between the biblical theology of unconditional grace and the conditional judgment passages to be more troublesome than does Ellis, the overriding clarity of radical grace as the substructure of all scripture is confirmed by Childs' canonical assessment.

The Bible sounds a clear and singular trumpet, whose notes convey singularly good news. It is the good news that first and uniquely exploded in the Judaic theological tradition and was captured pristinely by the Yahwist. It is the good news that God accepts us as and where we are for the sake of what we can, therefore, become. It is the good news about healing and wholeness for the pathological, inadequate, distorted, and lost persons of this world. It is the word about the only chance for the likes of us.

In sum, the theology of grace asserts that God is in the enterprise of healing. That grace, which is character rooted in God, is radical in its incisive thrust to the central locus of human pathology: the anxiety driven self-preoccupation that is both the cause and result of human alienation and of the world of sickness and sin that devolves from that alienation. That grace is unconditional, because it is not merely something God does but is, and hence it is an attribute and disposition inherent and inevitable to God. The Yahwist would have us apprehend, furthermore, that grace is universal in its scope and intent. The import is that humans are drawn by the Word to notice that the historical and empirical evidence available about the nature of God leads to a world view in which God's raison d'être, as humanly perceived, is the overt cultivation of the wholeness and wholesomeness of humans and of the whole creation.

That is the essential reason why this book attempts to explore the psychological consequences of a thoroughgoing biblical theology of divine grace. Hence also the functional title, *God's Grace and Human Health.*

A proper assessment of the theological idea and its psychological import requires some exploration of the problematic and pathological nature of the human setting to which grace speaks, an indication of how grace speaks to the human predicament, and a consolidation of the conceptual base for drawing out the psychological consequences.

The Human Predicament

Since humans first sensed the radical and generic nature of their spiritual and psychological fallenness, the most essential and universal human experience has been that of anxiety. As noted previously, Barbara Mertz expressed it as "our common human terror and our common hope."[3] Generic human anxiety is both systemic and situational to the human person. It is so radical in nature, that is, so close to the essence of human identity, that everything human is in some dimension shaped by it. Eric Fromm adequately describes the tragic side of its impact in human affairs in his book *The Anatomy of Human Destructiveness.*[4] John G. Finch has argued with considerable effect that generic human anxiety is also a potentially constructive dynamic in human growth.[5] Seward Hiltner has effectively related human anxiety and divine grace.[6] Mertz seems accurate, therefore, in relating generic human anxiety to both our terror and our hope.

Our Terror

The terror dimension of anxiety is readily identified by and in all humans. It ranges broadly from our struggle to come to terms with death and our omnipresent mortality, to such forms of exaggerated anxiety as those that are usually identified as, or produce, the plethora of pathologies we clinically speak of as neuroses. From the moment that the uterine contractions, signaling impending birth, begin, until the last gasp of life's breath in enfeebled old age, life offers an overarching set of anxiety-inducing threats to stasis, to goal achievement, to fulfillment, and to vital existence itself. The whole spectrum of life's experience-process may be comprehensively and definitely described as a conscious and subconscious endeavor at gaining control of one's destiny.

The native sense of psychological and spiritual fallenness universal to humans is surely rooted in that initial loss of the paradisiacal world of the womb, in which security is normally the overriding quality of experience. That loss is not experienced benignly but ingrains in our carlicst and most essential precognitive, psychospiritual experience a sense of the essential violent and tragic character of life. That humans ever achieve any genuine stasis and functionality after the birth trauma is really quite surprising and is evidence of the divine gift of the resilient force of life and will.[7] The beginning of terrors is really the experience of being torn violently and painfully from that setting to which we are adjusted, in that sense committed, and which we love systemically in the sense of being identified with, attached to, and dependent on it. Birth, therefore, means the loss experience, not merely of separation, but of separation perceived as alienation. That alienation is experienced in conjunction with an overwhelming sense of fragileness, vulnerability, and disenfranchisement. In terms of the classic dynamics of grief, that vulnerability is probably interpreted by the precognitive neonate as unworthiness. Our alienation from God and the godly, personally and as a community, reinforces all this sense.

It is of little surprise, therefore, that our sense of the authenticity of the biblical story of the Fall is so spontaneous. Genesis 3 accounts for, illumines, and interprets our most fundamental awareness: we are creatures of loss, a loss we experience and ultimately perceive as alienation and that feels like a state of powerlessness and unworthiness. Moreover, those experiences and perceptions lie chronologically, logically, and psychologically so close to our origins and our essence that we sense them as definitive of our identity. We are not just sick and lonely. We are alienated and lost souls.

For Adam and Eve, created at full bloom and ensconced in the garden of paradise, the story of the Fall describes a psychospiritual experience akin to the general human trauma of birth, combined with the postpubertal, oedipal entrenched process of adolescent disengagement from parents and home, with all its inherent separation anxiety, ambivalence, and endangered certification.

In short, our common human terror is that of being wrenched from our mother's womb and being unable to catch hold of our father's hand. The essential psychological and spiritual experience is that of being orphaned, and as is always the case with children who experience pain and grief-loss, we internalize that sense of lostness, personally and communally, as guilt. That guilt ultimately produces anger, because the rationality of that guilt is almost impossible to identify, and the anger reinforces our sense of alienation, producing our psychological and spiritual depression, distortions, patholo- gies, and hostile, inappropriate behavior. Here lies the threat of the loss of hope and of the meaningfulness and worthwhileness of things and is the engine driving our sin.

Our Hope

On the other hand, the separation experience of birth, as well as that of adolescent disengagement, brings with it the promise of hope. Both are pregnant with new possibilities. Birth brings a new breath of fresh air, as does the adolescent-young adult adjustment process and growth. In this the ontogeny of the person, so to speak, recapitulates the phylogeny of the cosmos.

In the biblical story, both the Creation and the Fall are oriented toward the future, both are driven by the dynamics of expectation, both are filled with the potential of new life and a new world. The first is paradisiacal, the second, tragic, but in a certain fundamental sense, both are part of the birth process of the universe. Both reach for the denouement of salvation and the completion and resolution of all things. The biblical story of creation, fall, and redemption is a historical paradigm of the universal human psychodynamic process of womb tranquility, birth trauma, adolescent disengagement, and maturation.[8] As in the paradigm, so in the psychology of the development of persons, the trauma of our genesis and the pain and risks of adolescence are drawn together into a comprehensive birth process from which the person comes, reaching consciously and subconsciously for the denouement of health and maturity with its healing resolution of things and its closures.

Now health and maturation, which I shall from this point comprehend in such terms as healing and wholeness, are achieved by stages, in fits and starts, with distortions, regressions and pathologies, hopeful surges and dead-end streets. This is not unlike the biblical paradigm in which God at various times in bits and pieces invested the fathers with salvation through the prophets and finally, in the end time illumined and healed us through his son (Heb. 1). The whole process in the human person and in the *Heilsgeschichte* paradigm reaches hopefully forward expecting fulfillment of the total potential of wholeness inherent in God's image bearers and in God's cosmic experiment.

The whole of life and history, therefore, can be described as the process of trauma moving toward hope, tragedy driving to denouement, pained and distorted life reaching for wholeness, anxiety wanting reduction, dissonance longing for resolution.

Anxiety Reduction and Human Health

Since the whole process of personal and cosmic function moves from incompleteness and pathology (lostness, distortion, and palpable illness) to maturity and wholeness (health, fulfillment, and palpable salvation), the efficiency with which this is accomplished depends directly upon the effectiveness of the reduction of distorting obstructions. In the biblical historical paradigm for the cosmos and the human community, the reduction of obstructions has to do with the removal of the bonds of chaos in Genesis 1:1, of primitivity and naïveté in Genesis 1 and 2, and of idolatry in the rest of Scripture. In the individualized psychodynamic odyssey of each person, the reduction of obstructions to wholeness involves anxiety reduction and thus transcendence over the pathology and distortions anxiety brings. Incidentally, in both the historical cosmic quest and the individual odyssey, wholeness is achieved ultimately *sola gratia* but not *soli Deo gloria*. Because grace is grace, the wholeness that it brings is, through incarnation, for the creation. History, the Bible, and sound psychotherapy are in that sense human centered. God, theology, and Christian psychology, when authentically perceived and expressed, are for and preoccupied with suffering persons and a suffering world (worlds).

Anxiety-reduction processes in the odyssey of personal growth may, of course, be constructive or destructive. I am convinced that all distortions, pathologies, and dead-end streets (self-destructive courses) in human psychospiritual development are the consequences of destructive anxiety-reduction mechanisms at the level of the psyche or at the level of social function, or both. Conversely, wholesome growth, health, and maturation are achieved to the degree that constructive anxiety-reduction mechanisms are introduced and utilized. Time and space do not permit an exploration here of the Fall as Adam's constructive or destructive anxiety-reduction mechanism for the anxiety laden hopeful quandary with which he struggled, regarding his potential to be like God, knowing good and evil. But that is a dimension of this matter that requires careful psychotheological analysis if one is to be biblically and theologically authentic. It is, therefore, treated at length in chapter 3.

Destructive anxiety-reduction mechanisms are those that produce inhibitory defense processes in human growth. Constructive anxiety-reduction mechanisms are those that enhance the openness for assertive risk-taking processes in human growth. The former obstruct, delay, distort, limit, or sicken and thus prevent the efficient move toward total self-actualization as an image bearer of God whose destiny it is to realize palpable fulfillment of the psychospiritual potential. Constructive anxiety-reduction mechanisms support, direct, reinforce, equip, embellish, and expand the human person and thus promote the efficient move toward total self-actualization. That realization of human destiny as the fulfillment of the full range of the psychospiritual potential with which God has invested us is the very definition of health and wholeness. Every function or behavior designed to bring that about is a healing act and the very definition of healing. All our sinfulness and our sickness is thus a falling short of the glory of God, because it is an obstruction of his glorious ambition for us: a falling short of the glory of real humanness. Functionality and dysfunction have their meaning against that backdrop.

The Role of Religion

The history of religion is the history of the human endeavor to devise functional anxiety-reduction mechanisms capable of managing situational and systemic angst. That long religious history divides easily into two radically opposite camps, shaped by differing strategies for anxiety reduction. The most prominent camp, historically, is the one shaped by the anxiety-reduction strategy of human achievement, measuring up to psychosocial standards of function that then authorize self-justification. This is essentially a strategy of self-justification by achievement of an ethical or psychosocial power position. It is self-centered and self-directed and tends to be legalistic and mechanistic. It is not growth oriented but status oriented, and since it treats only symptoms, the generic human anxiety is never effectively reduced. It is, in the end, self-defeating. It cannot cut through to the heart of the essential lostness and orphaned nature of human persons. It may provide a pseudowomb–return experience, such as some forms of institutionalized religion provide, but it never puts the grasping human hand back into the hand of our Father. In this strategy God remains the adversary who must be placated, outflanked, or intimidated and becomes a projection of the anxiety- and guilt-ridden psyche of the religionist whose unworthiness drives him or her to worship or work righteousness. This religious strategy for anxiety reduction produces and enhances psychopathology.

With one exception, religions throughout human history fall into this first camp, anxiety reduction by human achievement. They constitute a psychoreligious, power-play schema with all the potential pathology inherent in that set of defense mechanisms.

God's Grace

The only exception to this general psychospiritual tragedy of human history is the unique Judeo-Christian theology of grace. It is precisely the theology of the Yahwist, the Bible's first theologian, coming to flower in Jesus Christ and New Testament theology, that constitutes the only healing option. Only here is religion a constructive anxiety-reduction mechanism.

The theology of the Yahwist is such a healing option, because it cuts through to the heart of our essential lostness and orphaned nature. It is not a theology of self-justification but of unconditional divine acceptance. It is not a strategy for an ethical or psychosocial power play but a way of self-acceptance. It is not self-directed but goal-directed toward the completion of the whole person in Christ. It is not mechanistic or legalistic but dynamic, growth oriented, not status oriented. It mollifies some of the pain of our symptoms of psychospiritual unwholesomeness, but it treats the disease and the dis-ease of our alienation. It does not lead us back to the womb but puts our hand in the hand of our Father, not back to paradise but ahead to paradise. When properly mediated, the Yahwist's grace perspective heals human pathology in mind and spirit. It is, in fact, the most comprehensive and relevant psychological theory and practice ever conceived.

The Judeo-Christian God is not a threat but our consolation, whose name is Yahweh, the faithful one, who guarantees by his name and nature that he will always be for us what he has always been for humanity. That name is, therefore, a strong tower (security). "The righteous runneth into it, and is safe" (Prov. 18:10*b*). And *righteous* means, according to Micah and St. Paul, that person whom God has unconditionally accepted and to whom he has therefore imputed righteousness.

60

Unfortunately, superficial reading of the history of Judaism and Christianity will not confirm the radical uniqueness of that tradition of constructive anxiety-reduction strategy. By the heyday of Davidic Israel, a pagan legalism and mechanistic atonement theology were already rampant. Christ cut through to the essence of the grace theology, but by the fifth century of the Christian era the seeds of a pagan legalism were again sown; by the eighth century a sturdy growth was evident; and by the eleventh it had fruited. Luther grasped the essence once again, though scholasticism had demeaned Protestant grace theology two centuries later. At the personal level, even in the best times, popular religion has usually remained extensively threat-motivated paganism, despite the quality of the church's theology and ministry. Furthermore, in each generation there seems to arise a new form of Christian paganism that manifests itself in popular ecclesiastical movements that are essentially anxiety inducing or pathogenic in their anxiety-reduction strategies. The fastest growing churches tend consistently to be those that appeal to theologically untutored communities with notions that foster simplistic constructs of legalistic anxiety management—in essence strategies of self-righteousness and salvation by personal discipline.

That stands against the gospel of grace and the theology of the Yahwist. The substance of the Yahwist document itself is essentially the story of Creation, the Fall, the proto-evangelium, (in Genesis 3:15), the increasing disharmony in the universe of human affairs, the covenant with Abraham for the healing of the nations, the Exodus as enactment of Israel's chosenness, and the prospect of Davidic *shalom*. The theology hinges, of course, on Creation, Fall, and covenant. The central factor consistent throughout is the status of humanity. Adam appears on the scene as a special imager of the divine nature in a divinely ordered world. The God-imaging quality of Adam, in the creation story, describes the essential nature and character of humans. David J. A. Clines urges us to take this seriously enough to recognize that this doctrine elevates all humankind to the highest status conceivable, "short of complete divinization."[9] In that divinely ordered world, Adam is assigned the stature and status of compatriot of God. That status describes, not his essential nature as imager, but his role and relationship with God. He keeps the garden, names the animals, seeks a mate, receives Eve as God's gift for appropriate communion, and walks with God in the cool of the evening. His status is imputed to him by God, arbitrarily. The story never refers to Adam as son of God or child of God or servant of God. He is portrayed consistently as companion and compatriot. More-over, that status is a covenant status, not negotiated by Adam, but in the style of the Mesopotamian regents—imputed and guaranteed.

Part of Adam's wholesome character as compatriot of God is the quality of his imagination. He can imagine alternative worlds, alternative models of relationship, alternative perceptions of the good for which to quest, even evil perceptions of the good, and other anxiety-inducing possibilities, options and challenges. When Adam selected the alternative option of independence, the childlike harmony of his universe metamorphased into a dissonance and discordance that, but for grace, would have been deadly to the extent that it increasingly amplified Adam's alienation from the garden, the God-walks, his wife-talks, his own tranquility, and his own true destiny as a person in whom all the rich potential for wholeness could be actualized. The deadly dynamic in that independent course was the potential for overwhelming anxiety increase, to the point at which Adam would have been consumed by coping with his lostness, his inability to grasp again his Father's hand. Adam's status of God-compatriot seemed hopelessly forfeited and his course of behavior at fundamental odds with his own essential nature as an imager of God. *It was almost as though his God-imaging nature as independent creator was in tension with his God-compatriot nature of cokeeper of the garden.* That dissonance was the potential for sickness and death in the Fall.

The crucial issue, of course, is this: When Adam fell, God, despite his declaration "thou shalt surely die," refused to change Adam's essential status as God-compatriot. It was an arbitrarily imputed status. Now it is an arbitrarily maintained status. Adam's life now has about it the deadly pathological possibilities of overwhelming alienation, lostness, distortion, dissonance, sin, and sickness. But God came to Adam, sat where he sat, adopted the new circumstances of Adam's life as the new arena for the relationship, made clear immediately the unconditional nature of the compatriot status, and proceeded with the original business of Adam's move toward wholeness, completeness, growth, and healing. The ground rules seem somewhat modified, but only in terms of the new requirements for constructive anxiety reduction: the proto-evangelium and the reach toward Genesis 12:1-4 and 17:1-8, "I will bless you . . . you will be a blessing. . . . and by you all the families of the earth shall bless themselves."

The critical element of the theology of grace, throughout scripture, in consequence, is the essential inviolability of that status arbitrarily imputed by God to Adam and the whole human race. In the tragedy of our anxiety we perceive lostness and alienation. Out of that comes our sin and our sickness, psychologically and spiritually. From God's perspective, however, our status is unchanged. We are unconditionally affirmed as those destined for communion with God as a palpable frame for living. The gospel asserts that unconditionally certified status.

Human Health

The predicament of human existence, thus, is not our lostness but our perceived lostness. Our destiny is not that of achieving a successful power play to "get right with God" or get the right leverage with God. Our destiny is to accept and realize the benefits of our status: divine compatriots. The benefits are the relief of grace, the affirmation of our real selves, the unconditional acceptance of God's unconditional acceptance, and the celebration of our generic freedom from the need for generic anxiety: systemic ("Fear not, I am thy God") and situational ("Be anxious in nothing" "Take no thought for the morrow").

It is not surprising then, that St. Paul, in developing the rudiments of a Christian anthropology, should speak of "primordial man," "fallen man," and "the man in Christ," as Hans Dieter Betz points out. It is interesting that there is an apparent tension in Pauline anthropology between Paul's classical Greek humanistic roots and his classical Yahwist roots (cf. chap. 6). He worries greatly about the role of the law, the need for the suppression of the lower passion by the higher, the *sarx* held in check by the *psyche.* Yet he is radical in his "free grace theology" and the doctrine of imputed righteousness.

J. Christiaan Beker has just resolved that paradox in a delightful way in his book *Paul the Apostle,* by demonstrating conclusively that Paul never intends to write a systematic theology, not even in Romans.[10] Beker points out that Paul is always hammering out his theology, ecclesiology, and anthropology in terms of a very specific parish situation and that his thrust is always to demonstrate and celebrate the triumph of God in his grace in human life. Thus Paul can speak against the law and for radical grace in Galatians, where he is opposing the Jerusalem Judaizers, and for the law, as a certifier of Jewish priority though not superiority in Heilsge-schichte in Romans, where he wishes to settle a Gentile prejudice against Jews returning to the Roman church after their years of exile from that city. Beker points out that in Romans Paul is also wishing to catch the eye of the Jerusalem church to demonstrate that he is not separatist in his ambition to evangelize the Gentiles, as they may have gathered from his remarks to the Galatians. Paul's anthropology comes down to Yahwist theology and our imputed status in God's grace. That is the supremely relevant constructive anxiety-reduction mechanism of all history. It addresses the essential angst behind all psychopathology and spiritual disorder. It is the essential insight for healing and wholeness for humans.

Many attempts have been made to articulate the crucial nature and relevance of God's grace for human health. Most have been grounded and mired on issues of free will and divine election. It is a tragedy of near cosmic proportions that Calvinism and the Armenian tradition, after the breakthrough to grace in the Reformation, perpetuated the relatively superficial dialogue of the old Roman Catholic scholaticism while Anglicanism, the Anabaptists, and Methodism settled for a rather neurotic form of private pietism. These supplanted radical grace theology with a philosophically pragmatic or psychologically pragmatic form of muted grace, but muted grace is no grace. Compromised grace is pagan conditional self-righteousness. Even Bonhoeffer's "cheap grace" notion is a terrible misnomer that longs again for legalism and conditionalism. Grace is free, radical, unconditional, universal, or it is no grace, no good news at all, since it fails to get to the center of the pathology we are otherwise hopelessly locked into forever.

Some exciting recent studies of the biblical theology of grace require profound attention by psychologists today. Karl Barth, of course, broke the theology of grace out of the medieval prison of scholastic categories with his stimulating existentialist theology of election. James Daane's book *The Freedom of God* is a lucid step beyond Barth, in the tradition of Paul. It is a theology of the triumph of God, hammered out on the situational anvil of parish preaching.[11] Daane defeats scholasticism with its time bound God and a-Christian teleology by rooting election, as does Barth, in Christ and his historical function. Donald Bloesch says of Daane that he "persuasively argues that election is grounded in the *free decree of God* that is historical as well as eternal, and that has its culmination in Jesus Christ." More recently Neil Punt has given us a fine book entitled *Unconditional Good News.* [12] In it he argues that Yahwist and Pauline theologies import clearly that in Jesus Christ humanity is elect of God and that the redemptive consequences of that belong to all humankind, unless overtly and consciously rejected.

These, though they still do not go far enough in understanding grace, constitute great strides toward a thoroughgoing theology of grace that can illumine the essential nature of humans as God-compatriots. As the radical nature of that status becomes clearer to the theologians, their service to the psychologists and vice versa will substantially increase. As psychologists take with increasing seriousness (a) our fallenness as the source of human psychopathology, (b) the healing dynamic of incarnated grace, called by Carl Rogers, in his second naïveté, unconditional person regard, (c) the relationship between the clinical function and the divine paradigm behind it, and (d) the manner in which this essentially theological anthropology must shape theoretical and applied psychology if we are to handle humans authentically, the service of those psychologists to the theologians will be greatly enhanced regarding this very matter of defining and explicating grace. Perhaps Aquinas was right in his notion that what we have by faith in divine revelation, we would have had to come to anyway, if we had been able to track only the empirical evidence of human nature to its center.

One might object that my emphasis applies only to psychopathologies without associated chemistry disorder. I submit that the evidence is increasing that the two-way switching function of the hypothalamus urges the consideration that anxiety and lostness may even there be the pathogenic factor.

Secular and humanist psychology has provided valuable insight regarding symptomology, dynamics, and central disorders of the human psyche and soul. Secular descriptions of characteriological and personality disorders have achieved profound depth and precision. Strategies generally in use for management of pathologies have great value. Christian perspective, however, is indispensable in illumining the root cause and cure for our common human terror and our common hope.

CHAPTER 3

The Psychodynamics of the Fall Story

Introduction

The story of the fall of human beings into the sin of prideful disobedience recorded in the Hebrew scriptures is intensely intriguing from numerous points of view. Whether it is understood literally, metaphorically, mythically, or symbolically, the story provokes a spontaneous and universal sense of its authenticity. It is one of those stories that carries with it such archetypal quality that we sense at once that it touches, at the center, a generic truth of obvious human history and of vital personal experience. It speaks of the radical tragic distance between what we can imagine as our paradisiacal potential as persons and what we know as our often defeating and dissonant experience in real life.

The story is intriguing because, though it is woven into the fabric of Yahwist literature, it is, in fact, dependent for its formal elements upon archaic Mesopotamian sources. The role of the virgin, the tree, the fruit, the phallic serpent as tempter, and the like are imported with little alteration from pagan fertility literature. Though the story is not explicitly sexual, it is the story of a contest between two potential lovers for the allegiance of the virgin, a double seduction, the response of guilt, and the shame of sexual vulnerability and abuse.

The story is equally intriguing, for the manner in which the Hebrew editors attempted to adapt it for Yahwist use. Their key difference is the obvious literary effort undertaken to make the story fit and reveal something essential about the manner in which Yahweh relates to the impaired universe and the fractured human community as experienced existentially.

The function of the story

Related to this is the implication in the story of the general problem of evil. Clearly this pagan literary material is inserted into the fabric of the Hebrew scripture to service a Yahwist or Elohist theology in order to establish a base line for dealing with the problem as humans suffer it. The claim is unquestionably that a hubristic egotism led humans beyond their appropriate domain and landed them in such an erroneous perspective that God's design for nature, for communion, and for human relations seemed alien. The flowering shrubs began to look like thorns, the walks with God began to look like threat, and the complexity of relationship began to look like a thicket of unsortable confusion and pain.

The Fall story endeavors to account for the problem of human pain and the universal disorder. It attempts to explain why humans can conceive of aesthetic ideals but hardly create them, long for a perfect world but not fashion one, hope for genuine love but seldom express or experience it, remember and anticipate paradise yet sense it eluding us.

It is an intensely pathetic story of loss, grief, guilt, and shame. The pathos of the story is equally significant in revealing the essential nature of the universal human predicament, whether the story is understood as history or as myth. The literary characteristics strongly suggest, of course, that it should be viewed as a mythical pericope so invested with confessional theological content and import as to be profoundly true in what it says about our humanness, truer than mere historical reporting could ever possibly be. The truth it articulates is that of the general state of fallenness humans universally experience, expressed in the pervading distortion, debilitating anxiety, and apparent "wrongness" of human existence.

The story may be helpfully viewed as a theological myth, imported into the sacred canon by the Hebrew believers from pagan sources for the purpose of describing the psychological state of affairs they perceived to afflict humanity. They saw themselves and the human race as alienated, orphaned, and diseased. And they were, of course, correct.

If one takes the story of the Fall seriously as an element in a cosmic paradigm for general human psychological development, it becomes a crucial stage in human growth from the childlikeness of Eden to mature Kingdom building and cultural responsibility. In that growth process, the story plays the role that has equivalents in the human growth process of birth and adolescent disengagement. Those personal separation processes are normally fraught with significant anxiety. That anxiety is also evident in the story of the Fall in the reaction of Adam and Eve to events. There is significant anxiety with regard to the presence of the forbidden tree, to the perception of the possibility of making a forbidden decision, to the appearance of the tempting serpent, to the offer of the seduction of Eve, to her offer of seduction to Adam, to the threat of death, and to the guilt and shame of cutting loose from God. The whole fabric is expressive of intense anxiety.

In fact, the most interesting element is the plain implication of a significant and dangerous state of anxiety existing in the life and spirit of Adam and Eve before the Fall, when paradise was still intact. The recognition of significant anxiety before the Fall is crucial for insight into essential human nature as seen by the Hebrews. It implies the need in Adam, as he was created, for an anxiety-reduction mechanism that would make it possible for him to cope and to open up the door of his primitive and childlike life to real growth in terms of his God-given potential as a person with a growth-oriented destiny. As soon as God announced the presence and import of the forbidden tree, a state of anxiety existed in terms of Adam's perception that his potential destiny was open-ended and required decision-making by him and Eve. He recognized that he possessed the potential for change and for negative or positive growth. The anxiety increases in intensity as the story recounts Adam and Eve struggling with the essential decision about their unknown and challenging future. Moreover, the pressure of that anxiety is further increased as they contemplate, quite correctly, the possibility of being like God, knowing both good and evil.

It should not surprise us that the story describes Eden as anxiety laden. Stress in the pre-fall state, as described in this theological myth, is already evident much earlier. Adam is described as finding himself alone in the garden in a state of sufficient disequilibrium that he looked for a mate or companion among the animals. He found none adequate or appropriate. God noted the stress and anxiety and intervened by creating Eve as a help appropriate to his neediness. Obviously that means that she filled out some condition of lack and anguish in Adam and thereby reduced his stress and anxiety.

One can imagine that Adam had considerable stress from numerous directions in Eden: from the pressure of responsibility to keep the garden, responsibility to find companionship that was appropriate, to name the animals, to fashion a meaningful relationship with his wife, who ultimately chose a liberation course of independence and then seduced him into following her, presumably lest he lose her, and responsibility to obey and love God in a world where the manner of doing that held some ambiguity. The man was under pressure. His anxiety is not the consequence of his sin. His anxiety is clearly the consequence of his being a person with unexplored potential and possibilities. It is inherent to his nature and all human nature. It is inevitable to human existence, because of the nature of the potential for growth and the unfolding unknown that growth constitutes. The Hebrews saw that and related it to the potential in the world for the problem of evil. So they told the old Mesopotamian story in a new way and captured so precisely a truth generic to our existence that when we read the story five or six thousand years later or more, we find it touching the center of our predicament in some fundamental ways.

The story urges that all this stress and anxiety that Adam experienced was finally culminated in the enigma of what to do about the possibility of being like God. The story of the Fall, as the Hebrews understood it, describes the event and its decision as Adam's anxiety-reduction mechanism designed to free his psyche for further function, coping, and growth. The critical question, therefore, must be raised as to whether the event was a constructive or destructive anxiety-reduction mechanism for Adam and the human race. We ask the same question when we consider whether the painful process of birth and of adolescent disengagement is a constructive or destructive anxiety-reduction mechanism. It is important, because it will give us some clues as to whether we are to look at human alienation, pain, and anxiety and its consequences as difficult but inevitable stages in the evolution of persons and the human race or as an unfortunate aberration of a sinful or, at least, destructive type, as the Hebrews suggested.

Hiltner, Berry, and Clinebell

Seward Hiltner has contended persuasively that the story of the Fall is a metaphor of the human process of maturing to individuality and responsible agency as a person. He therefore urges that the story is a report on the human psychological process of asserting the will of the human person against the will of God. He claims that that act was necessary for humanity and is necessary for individuals, because saying yes to God in commitment to being a Christian and Kingdom builder has no meaning or content if it is impossible to say no.

Maturity for humanity, as for children, requires the ego strength and volition that forges the power and right to disengage in order to give significance to the intent or behavior of commitment. Hiltner's notion reflects the paradigm of adolescent disengagement and assumes that it requires a willful negative act, testing one's own strength over against one's parents, general authority, or pressures toward conformity. Without this disengagement there can be no growth.

C. Markham Berry suggests a similar perspective in pointing out that childhood is a stage of fusion with mother or parents. It moves progressively toward differentiation and achieves that with dramatic contrast in adolescence. Once the differentiation is successfully established and genuine individuality is achieved, there follows a process of return toward union, commitment, cherishing, and a new kind of fusion. Berry and Hiltner seem to support the contention of this chapter that the story of the Fall represents that growth step of differentiation and disengagement.

It is not quite as clear whether the story of the Fall describes a step taken in the best possible manner. Howard Clinebell appears to emphasize that the negative aspects of human nature are elements or stages in an evolutionary continuum of growth. One would imagine that he would find in the Hebrew fall story an interesting and entertaining metaphor, but one of little significance as to whether it represents a real disengagement from God for the sake of human growth toward discipleship or, in fact, comments in any other meaningful way upon the real human predicament. He appears to think in terms of humans moving more or less consistently along the growth line from primitivity, or childhood, to maturity, without the sort of psychological or historical discontinuity that the fall story or a painful adolescent disengagement represents, in persons or in the history of the race. He may well be correct.

Constructive or Destructive

If the adolescent differentiation is seen as paradigmatic of the fall story or vice versa, it is useful to ask whether Adam might have done it any better way. Does humanity need to express so much disjunction and experience, so much alienation and loss in order to achieve personhood and growth? Was it a constructive or destructive anxiety-reduction mechanism?

It is tempting to say that Adam chose the best course, and in view of his limited knowledge and experience, the only one he really had available. That is a way of saying that the loss and alienation we all experience from the loss of the womb and the adolescent individuation, together with the distortion in the intrapsychic and psychosocial world that drives our sickness and our sin, is virtually inevitable. As we grow, our limited knowledge, experience, and wisdom prevent us from choosing other than the painful and, at least temporarily, alienating course. Such an hypothesis would manage most of the relevant data neatly: This hypothesis implies that pain was inevitable, that the choice could not have been different if growth and maturation were to evolve out of the primitive and childlike naïveté of the Eden-womb.

It is clear, however that the formulators of the Hebrew recension of this myth intended to explain the problem of evil and human disorder by asserting that humanity made a bad choice. That does not imply that some decisive act by Adam to move him from naïveté to maturity was not necessary. Neither does it mean that nothing constructive toward real growth came out of Adam's decision. It only contends that his decision was a transitional act unnecessarily fraught with self-defeating pride, rebellion, and alienation. The Hebrews saw it as a destructive anxiety-reduction mechanism, insofar as they sensed it in those terms.

If one posits the notion that the fall story represents a destructive anxiety-reduction mechanism for Adam and, paradigmatically, represents the disorder and alienation in humans as an essentially destructive and self-defeating response to the generic anxiety of birth and differentiation, that does not erase the fact that the Fall has constructive, freedom-affording results for humans. Similarly, adolescence may be handled unnecessarily rebelliously by some teen-agers but lead out to a growth process that results in profoundly healthy relationships with parents, authorities, and traditions later on. Paul seems to imply something of this regarding humanity when he ties the primordial state of human "bliss" into a continuum with "fallen man" and the fruition of it all in the "new person in Christ."

The fall story represents one option for implementing the necessary and inevitable differentiation process. The Hebrews thought of it as a destructive option. The implication is that Adam might have exercised an equally growth-inducing act of will and ego strength by choosing, for independent and personal reasons, to affirm God's will and value system. That would have been as initiatory, independent, disengaging an act toward growth as disobedience proved to be. Presumably it would, moreover, have had less self-defeating, though adequately self-affirming, consequences. Moreover, the paradigmatic import for human history is the implication that the distortion, pain, alienation, and sickness with which humans have responded to generic anxiety through history were not inevitable elements of the growth process of the race. Humans have made many bad decisions: in the way they have apprehended God's real disposition toward them, in the way they have responded to quandary and ambiguity, and in the finesse with which they have affected their own psychological dynamics and destiny. Such decisions can be made wisely, redemptively, and faithfully, with healthier consequences.

Paradigmatically, the disengaging adolescent can achieve health and growth while choosing, as an independent act of will and ego, to affirm and follow the healthful values of parents, authority, tradition, or other sources of encouragement toward conformity. Indeed, that course, when expressing rather than compromising the child's own authenticity, may be far less self-defeating, inefficient, errosive of health, and painful than disengagement that strains relationships or maximizes confrontation, alienation, and grief-loss.

The story of the Fall is theological mythology that confesses the meaning of human pain and disorder in the face of a gracious and provident God who generously created and sustains us. Hiltner and Berry are correct in emphasizing the inevitable necessity of differentiation of human persons as persons from a womblike relation with God. It appears that the Hebrews were correct in implying that the disengagement could be less self-defeating and could affirm the perspective and value system that heals, rather than aggravates generic human anxiety and so sickens us. Perhaps Clinebell is really on the right track in de-emphasizing the cataclysmic and alienating dimensions of human fallenness while placing all the emphasis on the freedom for growth that humans as independent agents need and possess. His model handles the data in a way that implies that the Fall speaks of a revolution and that, however paradigmatic that may be of actual human experience, humankind has the alternative option of evolutionary growth response to generic human anxiety.

It is intriguing to consider the possibility of humanity in general, and children in particular, developing through a peaceful, relatively nonturbulent exploration of the possibilities for being like God/parents, knowing good and evil.

My initial perspective in wrestling with the fall story in

relationship to God's grace and human health was to conclude that Adam had no alternative. I was strongly inclined to the notion that turbulent and alienating process is inherent to adolescence and its disengagement as well as to birth, and so Adam's action seemed to me to be the only constructive anxiety-reduction mechanism he had available to free him toward health and growth.

I am indebted to my daughter Deborah Lynn for forcing me to rethink that. The idea at the center of this chapter is really her argument that the fall story represents an unnecessary, self-destructive form of adolescent rebellion. Presumably Adam's growth and differentiation could have developed tranquilly and evolved constructively to maturity, as in healthy and cherishing adolescents. That seems clearly to be what the Hebrews intended to say. What urged me to take a new look at the matter was the increasing success of Deborah's struggle to disengage by evolution, not revolution. She has refused assiduously to give up that course of cooperative exploration to maturity, even when I have been betimes less than useful to her constructive, exploratory growth. Disengagement by evolutionary and constructive anxiety reduction seems to be working for her definitively, and therefore for me also. It struck me in thinking of this that the odyssey of Jacques Cousteau's son must have been a little like Deborah's experience. Instead of running away to sea, literally and figuratively, as so many adolescents have in the last two decades, he went "down to the sea in ships" with his father and found wisdom and a beautiful new world. The metaphor is somewhat tortured by the untimely death of Cousteau *fils* in the ocean deep.

It is intriguing, in any case, to contemplate how things might have been in human history if the state of affairs in the human psyche and spirit were such as to permit and prompt a different mythic story in Genesis 3. What if the story could have represented humanity as reaching forward within the will of

God, for individuality, maturity, and wisdom, and for knowledge of being like God in comprehending the world inside out, in knowing God as he now knows us? Cooperative growth with God and exploration of the possibilities of human destiny in tranquility is not a story that rings true to the human experience of dissonance, alienation, and dis-ease, but it suggests a redemptive alternative that might have been from the beginning, if we were not so badly distorted by generic anxiety. It seems apparent that the invitation of grace to move into the growth mode of that redemptive option is really the whole issue of God's grace and human health.

God Imagers and the Fall

If we think of the fall story and of human distortion as destructive anxiety-reduction dynamics, a final significant question regarding human nature arises. In what sense do humans image God in choosing self-destructive or self-defeating courses?

The human behavior of will and ego over against power and authority reflects, and is possible because of, an essential dimension of God's nature in humans: the function and attribute of being independent creators and independent agents of our own destiny. In the story of the Fall and in real human experience of pain, disorder, distortion, and dis-ease, humans act as independent creators gone awry and as independent agents choosing self-defeating destinies. Those choices free humans to be persons and to grow, but they decrease the focus, efficiency, and gratification of that freedom and increase the dissonance, conflict, and errosive sense of alienation.

God, as independent agent, could also act in self-defeating ways but apparently does not. That is a credit to God's moral character as an independent moral being, not a result of his essential nature, as if he had no alternative.

This reminds one of the cynic's joke, Can God create a rock

that is so heavy God cannot lift it? The joke has greatly entertained the superficial and cynical secularist and unduly troubled the Christian philosopher. It is to the credit of the superficial Christian and the secular philosopher, perhaps, that it troubled neither of them much, both thinking it quite absurd.

It is, however, a profound question. The answer is not the one that Christian philosophers have given, i.e., that God cannot create a rock too heavy for God to lift since that is out of keeping with God's true character. The answer, I judge, is rather that God can very well create such a rock. He can do anything like that and any other sort of self-defeating thing, if he chooses to do so. Moreover, he can do it without ceasing to be God, contrary to the view of Christian philosophers. He would, of course, turn out to be a bad God in the moral sense of that term as well as in the social sense of the term. But he would not be a bad God in the ontological sense. He would still be God, and that is all that counts ontologically. In that sense it is not different for God than for humans who are bad morally and socially because they choose self-defeating behavior but remain humans in every ontological sense.

The crucial issue is that God has not created a rock too heavy for God to lift, so to speak, and has chosen not to engage in other self-defeating behavior because he has apparently chosen to behave with inviolate moral integrity. He has chosen to be true to his own nature and destiny. He is not merely locked into an inevitable moral quality because of his essence. He is free to choose, grow, explore, experiment, decide, and fail.

He has chosen not to do so. Not because of his essence, but because of his moral integrity and therefore, since all morality is ultimately aesthetics, because of his aesthetic integrity and sensitivity that cause his decision against self-defeating behavior. That is a matter of appropriateness and proportion. He is trustworthy, not merely as a being defined by logical or ontological inevitability, but as a being who is psychologically committed to holiness. Yahweh is not a Greek god in a pantheon of abstract qualities personified in archetypical figures. Yahweh is the Hebrew God, who chooses, acts, could err as Jesus could have at the temptation, and who decides not to do so. Yahweh decides to be moral, gracious, and sensitive.

Humans image God in the integrity of their choice processes. In that we are independent choosers, we image God and reflect his nature. We spoil the clear quality of the image when we choose inappropriateness and disproportion and defeat ourselves in our growth endeavors or needs.

Such was the case in the fall story. Such is the case in our daily failures to make sound, wholesome, and healing choices. Humans recapitulate the Fall daily. That is undoubtedly why we so spontaneously perceive the authenticity of that ancient myth.

CHAPTER 4

Contemporary Notions of Human Nature

It seems increasingly crucial to our work in the helping professions to clarify the concepts of humanness prevalent in our culture and in our psychological theory and practice. We encounter daily numerous bizarre and destructive models of who and what humans are in our clients, in our cultural value system, and in ourselves. In that regard, it seems quite important to acknowledge that the development of the Western world was influenced by a number of anthropological traditions, but supremely that of St. Paul.

Though Paul's anthropology is not always self-evident or easily ferreted out in the New Testament, he is the only New Testament theologian who developed anything approaching such a science. Paul himself was heavily influenced by three ancient traditions: the Mesopotamian, to which he is a contrast, and the Greek and Hebrew, which he absorbed. I should like to discuss at some length those sources of Western anthropology mediated through Paul and attempt to suggest how we encounter and can deal with them in our time.

Mesopotamian Anthropology

The Mesopotamian concept of human nature was essentially a demeaning one. These ancient civilizations had a peculiar record of having developed a world view basically rooted in a monotheism and proliferated in a secondary polytheism. The Sumerians, Chaldeans, Babylonians, and Assyrians were not remarkably different from one another in this regard. Marduk was the Babylonian progenitor of all things and functioned in terms of a subordinate hierarchy of gods, who enhanced and/or complicated his enterprises.

In any case, all these civilizations derived from this theology a concept of man as a creature who was demeaned and dehumanized by being trapped in an arbitrary, unfriendly, divine order of things. The gods made man from the inferior earthly substance of clay and then gave him the divine destiny of being servant to the gods to supply their needs and deliver them from menial survival tasks. Humans were of earthly substance with heavenly achievement demands. Man was trapped: by the very constituent nature of the gods as gods. Man as man was trapped: by the constituent nature of the universe.

Because humans were innately inferior, they could never escape the predicament of their inferiority. In the face of that, the gods unreasonably demanded of humans transcendent divine achievement.

It was in terms of that enigma that the Mesopotamians tended to explain the problem of evil: the problem of suffering, the problem of sickness, the problem of distortion. They held that the problem of psychological malady was the consequence of that impasse, and the more stoic and optimistic of them suggested that the only way to salvation was by a combination of three things: vigorous hard work, a good streak of luck, and the endeavor to outsmart or outflank the gods.

That notion of pseudo-optimism, of course, was good only for poets and philosophers. Just as in the history of the Christian faith in a secular world, apologetics has functioned as an impressive, sophisticated enterprise convincing only for apologists, so also in Mesopotamia that poetic notion of an outside chance of man's transcendence and survival was good only for the poets. In the end, there was a sinister kind of pessimism like Hegel's in his optimistic notion of the progressive, upward evolution of history. Schopenhauer and Nietzsche saw the determinism in Hegel and concluded that man was boxed in. They looked at Hegel's philosophy of magnificent progressive optimism and said, "The rub is that man is trapped in that magnificent evolution, and that is demeaning and pessimistic." So the Mesopotamian notion of the nature of man was essentially demeaning.

Greek Anthropology

In contrast, the Greek notion of human nature was infinitely more secular and was extremely optimistic. The Greek notion of man was a magnificent one. The Greeks went through an evolutionary process in which they dealt with this concept of anthropology in three different ways. If one had lived in pre-Homeric times, one would have had the inclination periodically, at least if one had had the strength or the money, to go to the oracle at Delphi and inquire of the gods about one's destiny. We remember that Oedipus, the unwitting aspirant to the throne of Thebes, went. The epic and dramatic literature of Homer, Hesiod, Aeschylus, Sophocles, and Euripedes repeatedly refers to their contemporaries and to the Greek ancients as going. Plato's dialogues and Socrates' reported discourses imply that it was a natural thing to inquire of Apollo at his oracle at Delphi.

When one went to the Delphic oracle, one entered the portals of the temple under an inscription that said: "Know thyself." Hans Dieter Betz points out that in pre-Homeric times that meant "Remember, you are just a man! When you go through these gates, be sure that you confess your status by saying to Apollo, 'Thou art.' " So there was a dialogue implied in the superscription. The pilgrim said, "O Apollo, thou art" and Apollo said, "Know thyself. Remember, you are merely human." Betz points out that "merely human" meant the same thing as "to err is human." That was a confronting experience for the Greek, but as is true of honest confrontation, it had in it the seeds of health.

The Greek who confronted himself in terms of the primitive meaning of Delphi was already coming to grips with his mere humanness, coming to grips with the fact that he was indeed the kind of creature in which it was native to err.

That sounds demeaning, but the implication is magnificent. As psychological healers and Christians, we should understand that better than anyone, knowing that if we come honestly to grips with our realities we are already a long way down the road to managing them constructively. Fortunately, that is what happened for the Greeks. It was the "universal education" impact of that primitive anthropology, mediated into the Greek cultural and psychological process by the oracle at Delphi, that produced the magnificent humanist experience that the Greeks achieved.

From that point on through the epic age to the Ionian scientific age of the sixth century B.C. and the golden age of Pericles, five hundred years before Christ, when Socrates reigned in his creative humanist thought, there developed a progressive metamorphosis in which the second stage was the Greek notion that to go to Delphi and read *gnothi auton* meant, not only "remember your mere humanness," but "accept your humanness compassionately and joyfully, not despairingly."

To be merely human was one thing. To be compassionately human was quite a new thing. It was a transcendent step magnificently beyond the primitive insight of honest self-acceptance. The Greeks discovered that the more they thought about that, the more significant man seemed and the less significant the gods seemed. That was a breakthrough of ingenious wisdom.

Greek theology began with a kind of animistic notion of God infesting every facet of nature. It was a primitive attempt to explain the mysterious powers present in the cosmos. That metamorphosed to the point where gods were given names, personalities, and domains. Poseidon was the god of the sea, for example. The problem of gods and power and threats in nature was lifted from animism to polytheism. So it was not just a matter of encountering an indefinable spiritual power when a mysterious wave suddenly sprang up out of the sea and overcame you and destroyed your goods and family. Now you could deal with Poseidon. Once you gave him a name, a biography, a personality, you could start to manage him. You could sacrifice to him before you left the Athenian harbor of Pireaus for the Peloponnesus. You could placate him. You could develop liturgies and rituals to manipulate him.

While Hebrew and Greek anthropology are remarkably different from their Mesopotamian precursors, they are also remarkably different from each other. The Greek notion of man seems to have evolved from primitive, demeaning anxiety about fragile humanness to the magnificent confidence of Socratic humanism. Apparently, as the Dorian migrants pulled themselves upward from the status of victims of the vagaries of nature to the status of masters of land and sea, from nomadic hunters to domesticated farmers and on to civilized urbanites, their dynamic struggle was to replace their fear of the mysterious spirit-filled unknown in nature with identifiable gods, whose personalities could be described and whose behavior could, therefore, be depended upon or managed. Then they struggled to replace these increasingly manageable and, therefore, laughable gods with heroic demigod-like men and finally with real man himself, in charge of his own destiny, secure in his unmystified rationality. The roles of a godlike Jesus Christ-like Prometheus, of a Heracles who civilizes by brute force, and of a Jason who civilizes by humane means are intriguing and wonderful, as one endeavors to understand the evolution of Greek anthropology. Tracing the moments when the awesome gods became humorous, the humorous gods became laughable, and the laughable gods scandalous and irrelevant, is itself a surprising and hilarious enterprise. Equally awesome and profoundly sobering is the visualization of how *fragile and demeaned man* became vigorous, clever, and durable man, how that man became honorable, estimable, and heroic man, and how that man became more moral than the gods, more humane than his creators, more masterful than the incredible, preoccupied, and irrelevant population of Olympus. That magnificent metamorphosis was the miracle of Greece.

Zeus, for example, was repeatedly pictured in venal pursuits unbecoming to the heroic and virtuous. He was perpetually chasing young maidens around the countryside, with his wife Hera scolding, maligning, and berating him. The gods first became identifiable, then manageable, then laughable, and finally, irrelevant.

As the gods became irrelevant, humans became increasingly significant. The significance lay in the fact that humans began to see themselves, not as merely human, but as compassionately and *transcendently* human. The Greeks came to the conclusion that it is not only true that "to err is human" but that to forgive is human. There is about human beings that potential for compassion that is ultimately redeeming in their view.

Finally, the golden age of Greek humanism arrived, with the Greeks achieving the notion that humans were not just compassionately human. Humanity was magnificently human. So magnificently human was humanity, they concluded, that the whole of human destiny was in human hands. The slogan of the golden age was "Man is the measure of all things."

In that process, of course, the Greeks had to deal also with the problem of evil. They dealt with the problem in nature and the universe by saying that the problems of pain and suffering and evil were only apparent. "What we used to think were the whims of the gods afflicting us out of avarice, insensitivity, or ignorance, are really only the normal, natural processes of nature. The only real evil is in man's inhumanity to man."

The Greeks endeavored to manage that in the humanistic age by identifying the two sides of human nature: magnificent human rationality and unfortunate human animality. These constituted the magnificent and the malignant in humanity for the Greeks. These represented the contest between the mind and the body, the *psyche* and the *sarx,* the spirit and the flesh. The destiny of rational man was, therefore, seen as the responsibility to subject the *sarx* to the dominion of the *psyche,* to place the flesh under the control of the mind or spirit, human rationality. This primacy of the intellect and the implied triumph of the spirit over the flesh, the higher passions over the lower, finally was conceived by the Greeks as the road to salvation.

The centuries that follow the golden age, of course, tell an interesting story of despair and disillusion. Man as god proved unable to manage his "god-ness," or even his goodness. Existentialist loss of meaning set in and brought on a wholesale lunge into primitive mystery religions, then bizarre supernaturalism followed. That unfortunate course is similar to the pattern of history from the humanism of the nineteenth-century Western rationalism to existentialist despair with Camus, Sartre, and Kierkegaard at the turn of the century and on to the current preoccupation with astrology, karma, and reincarnation in the West.

Hebrew Anthropology

The third significant anthropological tradition in the ancient world that fed Paul's concept of human nature is the Hebrew one. It is a subtle, simple, majestic tradition. It is essentially the story of mankind in the Old Testament. In very brief summary, it is the story of Yahweh, the covenanting God, embracing sons and daughters.

The story of man in Hebrew thought may be looked at from various directions. First, it is a unitary notion throughout. The Hebrew anthropology knows nothing of the division of body, mind, and spirit. It knows nothing of the tension or contrast the Greeks saw between flesh and spirit, *sarx* and *psyche*. For the Hebrews, man is one. It is not so much the body that requires redirection or suppression; it is not so much a matter of dominance of *soma* or *sarx* by *psyche*. It is out of the heart that the issues of life flow, i.e., out of the center of one's being. Man is person to the Hebrews, person and personality, and must be dealt with as a totality. This was so true for the Hebrews that they had a great deal of difficulty conceptualizing death. There is no reference in the Old Testament to a specific experience of a soul going to heaven at death, or going to hell. The Hebrews continued to talk about death and Sheol as an undifferentiated and undefined matter. One died and entered into a different kind of existence, but the concept of differentiation was not complete. One reason was that they had difficulty dealing with the notion that a person could be split; that when the body is dead, there is something else that goes somewhere. They thought of persons as one. The unitary concept of the person is the first essential principle in the Hebrew notion of human nature.

The second element in Hebrew anthropology, detailed in chapter 2 is the concept of the co-regent and co-worker with God in God's world. That is a majestic notion of human nature and role that stands in contrast with the human predicament in the world of secularity and pain.

Paul picks up the Hebrew notion of man and deals with it in three terms. He speaks, in effect, of what might be called the primordial man: man in the pristine state of conformity to

God's primeval design. He speaks secondly of fallen man, as depicted in Romans 1–5, where the contrast is boldly focused between God's design for man and what man ends up being. Finally, he speaks of the man in Christ.

It seems clear that when Paul said he was a Hebrew of the Hebrews, one of the things definitely implied is his heavy dependence on this Semitic Hebrew anthropological model and tradition. Fortunately, or perhaps unfortunately, for Paul and his own peace of mind and psychointellectual integration, he was caught up in a world where he found himself dealing with a significant tension between the humanist notion of man from the Greek anthropological mainstream and the theistic notion of man from the Hebrew mainstream.

Paul was not toying with humanism, although from a certain perspective his anthropology might be described as a Christian humanism. He was trying to integrate the unitary Hebrew notion of man and the Greek notion of man, which were at war within him: *soma/sarx* and *psyche,* the lower and higher passions.

Ridderbos deals with the problem of *soma, sarx,* and *psyche* in Paul and points out that the apostle ends up with a Christian anthropology in which the Hebrew and Greek traditions are reasonably and adequately integrated. There remains, however, a tension, which comes out in the following manner, as regards our concerns as Christian counselors.

Paul consistently wishes to say that primordial man, in the face of the predicament of fallen man, always exists as a kind of ideal. Salvation comes, nevertheless, only when we transcend both the pristine state of Eden and the state of our brokenness, alienation, fallenness, and our pathology and become persons in Christ. What does that mean for Paul? It means for persons, always in the context of the community, the church, to experience the relief of Christ: to be in the way of Christ and, in that certain sense, to incarnate Christ, to be the Body of Christ. It means for a human to be one in whom Christ can be seen to function.

However, while trying to hold firmly to that on the one hand, Paul deals with the problem of the disorder in human nature in terms of the Greek categories: flesh and spirit. "There is a war within me," he says. It is a tension between *psyche* and *soma/sarx*. That tension Paul sometimes tends to resolve as the Greeks did: the management and suppression of the flesh by the dominance of the mind, rationality, or spirit. Clearly it was a problem for Paul to work out.

In the end Paul is really sure that the only salvation is in Christ. It is a gift. It is unconditional. It is free and unmerited. At the same time, there is a discipline implied in that gift of grace. The discipline implied is the management of the lower passions by the higher, a strictly Greek notion.

Contemporary Culture

We are dealing in our world with essentially four anthropologies that function in our cultural, social, and psychological processes. In our own minds, in the minds of our colleagues, both Christian and secular, and in the minds of our clients, undoubtedly even a more crucial fact, these four models shape life.

One of these anthropological models prominent right now is the Mesopotamian—that devastating demeaning notion of man as trapped. It seems to me that Schopenhauer can be thanked for that. Hegel conceived of the whole of the human experiment in a very optimistic way, saying that history is the interplay of the thesis, antithesis, synthesis; and as a consequence of that dynamic, history is moving progressively both forward and upward to the kingdom of God.

Schopenhauer perceived that the problem with Hegel's notion was that "man is trapped." Out of that came the despair of Nietzsche.

Man is trapped. The existentialism of Camus and Sartre, the general philosophical tone and temper of the twentieth century, the attitude of many of our patients and companions is really the Mesopotamian anthropology: the demeaning despair of the trapped human.

The second prevalent model of man is the notion of the Greeks. That is the incredible optimism of the secular man who is the measure of all things, whose destiny is in his own hands. All he needs to do is to get sufficient education, gain sufficient insight, develop sufficient rationality, or receive sufficient psychoanalysis or psychotherapy; and he is saved for himself and for his creative destiny.

There is something wonderfully entertaining and attractive about that model. I could very easily be a humanist. I could quite easily be a secular humanist. I like the idea of being a Christian humanist. That means I am always tempted with that second model of human nature.

The third model of man is a secularized Hebrew notion, the notion of a human being as a unitary phenomenon, who has all the prerogatives and possibilities of his meaning and destiny written into the structure of his individuality. This is a hybrid of the idea of humans as magnificently pre-programmed by genetic design on the one hand, and the radical notion of the virtue of selfishness, on the other. To be healthy and human means to be more totally and authentically individual and thus be more wholesome for everybody. Ayn Rand is a champion of the latter notion, especially in her book *Virtue of Selfishness*. She suggests that the whole notion of Christian agape is really a subterfuge. If you really want to be wholesome for the world, you must cultivate creative selfishness. If you are really good for yourself, then you are really best for everybody else. The idea of genetic pre-programmed humans is reinforced by the influence upon anthropology of the new inquiry into the DNA chain and the possibilities of genetic management or manipulation. There is something so close to the truth about both facets of this model that it really is a subtle and tempting possibility. Both notions have a significant dimension of truth in them.

The fourth anthropology is the Christian model. I do not agree totally with Ridderbos that Paul successfully integrates the Greek and Hebrew anthropologies and formulates a thoroughgoing Christian anthropology. I am much more inclined to feel that Paul might profitably have stayed closer to the Hebrew Yahwist model of human nature. The Christian concept of human nature has at least these dimensions. First, it requires that we take our human predicament seriously, i.e., that we acknowledge that the problem of human beings is a radical problem. The problem of our disorder, of our disorientation, our brokenness, our alienation, our proclivity to losing the sense of the meaningfulness of things cuts right through to the very center of our existence. In the final analysis, our problem is, not how many sins we have committed, but who we know ourselves to be. It is a problem of identity. So that a Christian concept of man is the concept of man fundamentally disordered but possessing two crucial redemptive potentials. The first one, prominent in the Hebrew notion, is the native, healthy, integrating urge of life itself to health, to wholesomeness, to what we are designed by God to be. The second is the possibility in Christ to become not only a compatriot of God, but a healer of his world, through the experience of God's gracious acceptance. That is, we can become the incarnation of Christ in the present moment. We can be the Body of Christ. In that sense, we can be Christ for others, not just compatriots of God, but God in Christ, present through us for a needy world of fractured humans.

We encounter all these models and their consequences continually in our interaction with clients. If we fail to clarify the model of man in these terms, we tend to lose efficiency in achieving healing. One of the great disorders we constantly encounter and should recognize is the disorder of identity. Some of the worst human suffering is observed in the person who cannot conceive of himself or herself as one beloved, a potential object of graciousness. Yet that is the fundamental element in the Christian concept of human nature.

In Jesus, grace meant unconditionally accepting the adulterous woman, ordaining the denying Peter, embracing Judas. So when Jesus said, "As the Father sent me into the world, so send I you," he must have meant that we should deal in the Christian notion of man, i.e., as the purveyors and potential receivers of that experience of grace.

CHAPTER 5

Implications for
Psychology Theory Development

Introduction

The biblical story as paradigm of the human psychological odyssey asserts an inherent union of experience in our history and in God's. That import centers in the realization that life for God, as Spirit, and the life of the human psyche cut across each other at such a substantive level as to effect the description/definition of both. To employ theology requires a useful anthropology. To employ anthropology exhaustively places one finally in theology. One must come at each with an eye to the other. The same can be said, at a lower key, about the science of any other facet of the cosmos, as well.

So religion is barren without a comprehensive appreciation of creation, and creation at center can only be understood religiously. The natural and social sciences must inquire finally of theology. Theology must listen and speak to the natural and social sciences. Psychology is an applied social science with a base in the natural sciences, just as are medicine, education, and preaching. Psychology properly exercises the stewardship of its mandate by collecting data, formulating theories for accounting for the data, and applying the interpreted data to concerns in psychotherapy. Theory development is a religious act. It hinges upon one's *pou sto* and upon one's *Weltanschauung*, i.e., an act with a faith assumption behind it.[1] Theory development is one of the key intersections of natural science and theology, and that intersection shapes and constrains everything in the social sciences.

This chapter addresses some of the implications of a thoroughgoing grace theology for psychology theory development. It will emphasize the problem of the intersection of theology and psychology and the import of a Christian anthropology for responsible development of personality theory. The chapter will then consider the problem of a theology of illness, and the psychological theory of healing, wholeness, and redemption, which will be developed in chapter 6 on clinical concerns.

The Intersection of Theology and Psychology

Egbert Schuurman, a professor of Christian philosophy at Eindhoven Institute of Technology and lecturer in the philosophy of culture at the Free University of Amsterdam, recently published a book entitled *Technology and the Future: A Philosophical Challenge*. This book might be considered as a model for handling the issue of the relationship between the claims of Christian confession and the scientific enterprise. Schuurman does not follow the pattern of those who reject technology for society, or of those who look toward technology as the avenue of salvation for our culture.

I advocate an integration of Christian belief and philosophical (or scientific) thought. Such an integration allows a fresh light to fall on the problems posed by the transcendentalists and positivists and on their suggested solutions to these problems . . . their views are mutually contradictory. The one group is oriented to human freedom, the other to technological power. Freedom and power exist for them in an eternally unbridgeable dichotomy. Furthermore, these secularized motives have clearly distorted technological development. Only when freedom and power are brought into harmony—and this is only possible through an acknowledgement that created reality, including humanity, is not self-sufficient—does a meaningful, liberating perspective for technological development open up.[2]

Professionals concerned with the intersection of theology and psychology must, of course, follow a similar course in a similarly sensationalized and politicized setting, since that is the arena into which psychology has been thrown during the last two decades.

After a profound analysis of both extremes, Schuurman develops the basis for the distinctive contribution that technology can make. As in his previous book, *Reflections of the Technological Society,* he presents an interplay between modern philosophy and modern technology.[3] Christian psychologists must do the counterpart of that in our discipline.

Stanley L. Jaki, a distinguished Benedictine priest with doctorates in both systematic theology and physics, has taken a similar approach, somewhat closer to the problem of the relation between psychology and theology. He has recently published *The Road of Science and the Ways to God,*[4] demonstrating from the history of science the key role that a rational theology has had in the rise of science and its plethora of applied achievements. He confirms Francis Bacon's choice remark upon the obverse of that argument, namely, that a little philosophy (science) leads one to atheism, but profound (comprehensive and exhaustive) philosophy leads one to theism.

In an even more recent volume, *Cosmos and Creator,*[5] Jaki explores the connection between the anthropology that functions in the natural and social sciences handled from secular perspectives, and from a Christian perspective in anthropology. Jaki promises to illumine and enhance our quest to understand the interface of the psychological and theological sciences. His thrust, like Schuurman's, assumes the essential legitimacy of the secular scientific quest for truth, expects productivity from what the natural-social sciences and the theological sciences may bring to their intersection with each other and from their dialogue, and considers that the crucial element will be the quality of the perspective each offers regarding the other, and regarding their subject matter.

The evangelical dialogue regarding the "integration" of theology and psychology, which has characterized the last decade, has illustrated both the difficulty and potential productivity of the quest for and effective intersection of the two. Rodger Bufford pointed out that "within the area of the relationship of psychology to Christian faith, the term integration has come to refer to efforts to portray psychological principles, including theory and empirical data, as consistent with evangelical theological understanding of the biblical texts."[6]

With that perspective in mind the evangelical quest largely separated itself from the sturdy enterprise of Boisen and Hiltner and their promotion of the Clinical Pastoral Education movement and more recently the development of the American Association of Pastoral Counselors. That separation has produced a regrettable loss of seminal and productive dialogue throughout the general Christian community regarding the relationship of psychology and theology. The reasons for the separation are simple, interesting, even humorous, and certainly understandable. The preference of the Hiltner-Boisen movement for a more philosophical theology and for Freudian psychology put evangelicals on the defensive. That led the liberal camp to question the sophistication of the evangelicals theologically. The intriguing fact that evangelicals were, meanwhile, training themselves increasingly as clinical psychologists while the Hiltner-Boisen professionals were theologian-pastors, raised some question in evangelical minds regarding the professional integrity or sophistication of their counterparts. That peculiar, nearly comical, twist in perspectives and pedigrees kept the two camps from helping each other until very recently.

With the increased interest in the last four years of persons like Seward Hiltner in such professional enterprises as the Christian Association for Psychological Studies and with the increased openness of evangelical professionals to the gains made by progressive and liberal biblical and systematic theologians, there is genuinely optimistic prospect for the decade of the eighties to become profoundly productive, expanding the scope and depth of the investigation of the relationship between Christian confession and psychology theory development. The complete spectrum of the Christian community may be comprehended in the dialogue and in the intellectual and spiritual ferment it will surely stimulate. Hiltner's *Theological Dynamics,* recently reissued in paperback by Abingdon, will be a significant contribution to the dialogue if evangelical professionals attend with diligence and appreciation.

In 1977 H. Newton Malony produced an extremely useful tool for exploring the issue of intersection and integration, a "Beginning Bibliography in the Integration of Psychology and Theology." Unfortunately it has not yet been published, and I have a great sense of personal urgency for commending or assisting Dr. Malony in bringing his crucial research tool up-to-date and making it formally available to the general scholarly world. I should think that needs to be done this year, again in 1985, and once more in 1990.

In his 1977 bibliography, Malony listed 532 sources relating directly to the matter of integration of psychology and theology. He admitted that the list was not exhaustive. In fact, it lacked substantial items from what has been referred to as the liberal school in Christian concerns, but it constitutes a significant base line for the history of scholarship in this area.

Predictably, much of the really creative and definitive material on the intersection of theology and psychology has been published since 1977. Kirk Farnsworth brought the early years of this struggle into focus in 1974 with his article in the *Journal of Psychology and Theology* called simply "Embodied Integration."[7] He appealed along the lines of Francis A. Schaeffer's thought, for the avoidance of forcing a perceived dichotomy between faith and science into a contrived unity.[8] He raised the crucial point that God speaks in nature and in grace, and presumably without forked tongue. Farnsworth asked for embodiment in the Christian professional of sound theology and sound psychology on the assumption that thus both will come out with sophisticated application and scientific integrity.

I have argued previously along these lines but pressing the point that the very term *integration* is problematic in that it suggests a conceptual model in which theology and psychology are disparate and alien and need to be force-fitted together in order for a Christian psychologist to function responsibly. I suggested disposing of the term and its conceptual model in favor of a perspectival model in which each scientific discipline is approached from the perspective of the other and hence is formed and informed by the other.[9] Schaeffer's point is critical here.

> If both studies can be adequately pursued, there will be no final conflict . . . it is important to keep in mind that there is a great difference between saying the same thing in two different symbol systems and actually saying two different exclusive things but hiding the difference with the two different symbol systems. What the Bible teaches where it touches history and the cosmos and what science teaches where it touches the same areas do not stand in a discontinuity.[10]

Clinton W. McLemore advanced the quest for the intersection of theology and psychology with his article "The Nature of Psychotheology: Varieties of Conceptual Integration."[11] He suggested four loci of intersection: (a) applying the findings of psychological science to Christian living, (b) describing the correlation between cosmological and ontological implications disclosed by psychology and theology, (c) exploring the relationship between Christian gospel and human development, and (d) using sophisticated psychology to give apologetic force to Christian theology. McLemore struggled with the term *integration,* and suggested handling the issue by calling it the enterprise of psychotheology.

P. Clement and N. Warren suggested most helpfully in 1973 that the intersection of psychology and theology may be located in four areas, differently described than those of McLemore: a conceptual theoretical level, the research and data base level, the clinical experience level, and the intrapersonal level.[12] They suggest that persons with different talents or professional proclivities may work at a problem at any one of these levels, essentially apart from the others.

Kenneth Mathisen contends that the conceptual theoretical level of intersection must be thoroughly established as a basis for work on all the other levels.[13] C. Markham Berry argues that the description of the intersection at the data base must be thoroughly established before good work can be done at the conceptual theoretical level.[14] I am tempted to call Mathisen a Platonist and Berry an Aristotelian. The truth is probably somewhere in between, that is, Christian theologians and psychologists need to deal exhaustively with both the data base and the theory, not as separated or of differing priority, but as critically interactive in formulation of theoretical constructs and research (data handling) designs as well as the interpretation process. Koteskey agrees with Mathisen, Larzelere and Collins[15] agree with my position suggested immediately above.

Robert Larzelere recently proposed six levels of scientific inquiry to show how each could compliment the others. He notes that theology and psychology may be seen to interact at the levels of world view, general proposition, linkage, specific proposition, hypothesis, and data base. He describes the six respectively, as dealing with the following concerns. The world view level concerns basic assumptions and values; general theories and models are treated at the general proposition level; linkage deals with inductive/deductive logic; specific models and laws are the work of the specific proposition level; hypothesis-forming treats generalization from the data to research models; the data base level concerns collection and screening of raw information.[16] This approach confirms but does not really go beyond the emphasis of Clement and Warren indicated above, namely, the intersection at the theoretical and research levels. Moreover, Larzelere virtually omits consideration of the applied clinical level, except as a data-gathering locus.

Larzelere's model, in any case, actually comes down to three levels of intersection of theology and psychology: theoretical assumptions, research methodology, and data base. Those seem to me to be, in addition to the applied arena of clinical experience, the essential areas of concern in this matter and the loci at which constructive work can be done in relating our faith to our professions and the science of theology with the science of psychology (cf. fig. 7). Moreover, these four always must remain interactive, mutually forming and informing the shape and perspective of the others. Then we can be integrated persons, who are sophisticated Christian believers and sophisticated psychologists. At the level of personal function, I think, is the location where the term *integration* is relevant. A correct perspectival model of theology and psychology can produce integrated Christian professional persons (cf. fig. 8).

Figure 7

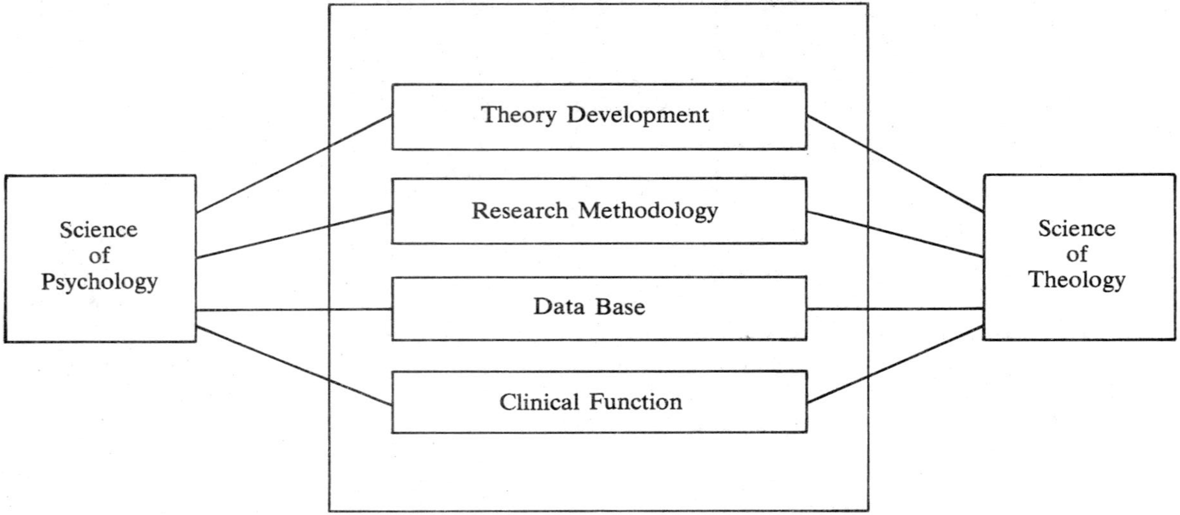

Science of Theology

Theory Development

Research Methodology

Data Base

Clinical Function

Science of Psychology

Arnold De Graaf of the Institute for Christian Studies in Toronto has made a valuable point here.

> My proposal with regard to the question of integration is that we approach this problem from an opposite perspective. Instead of a tension or duality, let us assume that there is an integral unity and harmony between our faith and our feelings, between findings of theology and of psychology, between our view of the person and our experience. Let us also assume that human nature is an integral, unified, centered spiritual creature . . . then our task with regard to integration is not so much to *construct* a unity as it is to *discover* the integral unity that is there. . . . Then we are to let the phenomenon that we experience *reveal* its integrality.[17]

Since, then, theology and psychology intersect at the level of theoretical assumptions, research methodology, data base, and clinical application, forming and informing one another at each level, and since the subject of study at each level is the human person, it is apparent that the phenomenon in which the intersection of theology and psychology is discerned and realized is the anthropological model that functions or is forming at the point of intersection. One might say that an auto engine runs on gasoline in gaseous form and on oxygen and hydrogen molecules in gaseous form. One might further explain that the engine works because in it these two gaseous elements, gasoline and air, intersect, forming and informing each other. For an especially interested student, one might go on to explain that intersection is evident at various levels, at the level of the carburetor and at the level of the combustion chamber in the cylinder. One might continue with an even more precocious student to suggest that the specific component where the intersection of gas and air is enacted is the venturi tube in the carburetor.

I see something like that as the role of that anthropological component in each of the loci of intersection of theology and

Figure 8

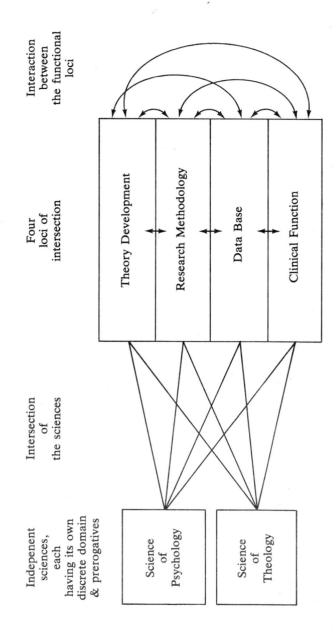

psychology, in which the concept of the nature of humanness is functioning or forming. The integrality of things, as De Graaf would have us speak of it, is realized then, in terms of the anthropological authenticity we experience regarding the impact of psychology and theology in our assumptions and theory development, our research methodology and hypotheses, our data collection sources and designs, and our clinical function and fruitfulness. That authenticity experience comprehends both speculative and empirical experience (cf. fig. 9).

So, sound pursuit of the inevitably religious enterprise of psychology theory development, informed by our best insights from speculation, research, empirical evidence, and clinical experience, must always be a conscious and creative quest for a warrantable anthropology. If we can achieve a warrantable anthropology, we will be able to formulate authentic personality theory, theories of pathology, and theories of healing, wholeness, and wholesomeness.

The key problem for developing a warrantable anthropology within the ferment of the intersection of theology and psychology is one of establishing the criteria for judging truth as truth and apparent truth as falsehood. This book is not going to solve that problem but, rather, focus it and hold out for two critical elements in the solution. Further study will be absolutely necessary at precisely this location if the dialogue regarding science and the Christian faith is to move ahead. We have danced all around this issue but have not resolved the impasse. We must do that shortly, or our digestion of the relation of theology and psychology will again be constipated as it was in 1974.

Let us push the matter onward with the following observations. First, the scientific method, classically conceived by Aristotle, Aquinas, and Francis Bacon, is indispensable to our investigation of both the theological and

Figure 9

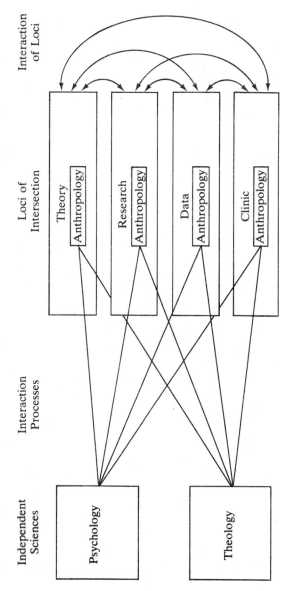

The anthropological concept that is forming or funtioning in each locus of intersection is the actual junction element that constitutes the cite of intersection.

psychological sciences if we are to obey the first principle of Christian scientific theory development, viz., that our theories must be warrantable theories. Warrantable means "as thoroughly in conformity to the whole truth at our disposal as we have the resources to make possible."

The second critical element in the solution of the problem of norms and criteria for adjudging truth is awareness that truth *(aletheia)* to the Greeks was one thing, and to the Hebrew Yahwist and that whole tradition it *(emeth)* was quite another. The modern world of science and technology has been uniformly dominated by the Greek notion of truth, with its implied rational empiricism. Only lately has a mind-set developed in the West that seems to long for the Hebrew form of the truth.

Jack Boghasian[18] has recently emphasized the import of this issue and leads us to Boman's excellent *Hebrew Thought Compared with Greek.*[19] For the Greek, truth is what is evident, clear, seen. For the Hebrew, truth is what is dependable, faithful, trustworthy. The Greek notion deals with objectivity, the Hebrew with subjectivity. Boghasian says, "Hebraic truth is not metaphysical but rather characterological. Indeed it is interpersonal."

It is not surprising that in the world view of the Yahwist theologian the idea that God had covenanted with humanity under the name *YHWH* was central. "I will be whom I have always been," the God who upholds the human status of the God-compatriot and who will never abrogate that status under any circumstance. Neither is it surprising that the Hebrew tradition was not recorded in philosophical treatises like those of the classical Greek humanists. It was preserved, instead, in the very personal record of the mighty acts of God in Israel's particular history. For the Greeks truth was evidential and hence static through time, inherent in creation. For the Hebrews truth was dynamic, unfolding through time, implied in creation, but realized in the perpetual process of redemptive and providential re-creation. Greek truth required standing outside the system and observing the evidence and logic of it. Hebrew truth required assuming a stance inside the system to hear or feel the confirmation of it exuding from experience. Even the word of the prophets was ultimately useful precisely in terms of personal encounter with the Word incarnated in a person, the Man from Nazareth, who, for those who walked with him and were touched by him, quite unexpectedly showed up to be the Christ of God.

To establish adequate criteria for assessing the data of experience or of speculative reflection or of logical deduction as truth, it is imperative that we devise sound strategy and tactics for applying the constraints of the scientific method to the Hebrew type of truth. In the last twenty years the field of psychology has moved the modern world substantially in the direction of conceiving of truth in the Hebrew fashion. Abraham Maslow's insistence upon the truth value of the world of the feelings has revised our culture radically. His posture implies a set of philosophical assumptions to the effect that all truth is not objective, to be seen best from the outside in, but is just as often subjective, to be appreciated best from the inside out. Carl Rogers' client centered therapy is an approach devolving from a specific anthropological view that truth is psychological and personal in the Hebraic sense.

It must be clearly the case that alone, neither the Greeks nor the Hebrews were right about the truth by themselves, but both are correct when held together. It is important to note that Paul tried hard to do that, especially in his anthropology.[20] It is even more intriguing that Aristotle, the father of the scientific method, in his move from Platonic idealism to rational empiricism, was aware of this crucial insight. He preferred to think of himself, not as a philosopher, but as a psychologist. However, he never worked out this issue or moved beyond the classical Greek view of truth. It is likely that if Western ecclesiastical development had followed

Augustine, however, as the Eastern church did, instead of Anselm and Aquinas with the unresolved problem of Aristoteleanism, the modern era would have been shaped by a Hebrew notion of truth and method, rather than Greek. That Hebrew posture is still evident in the Eastern church's preference for theology as celebration, a psychological phenomenon, versus the Western Church's preference for theology as proposition, a logical phenomenon.[21]

The force of contemporary psychology and the oriental notions of truth impinging upon us from Eastern religions are moving American culture toward a balance between the Greek and Hebrew perceptions of truth. That will make us more able to employ sound anthropology and finally resolve the quest for the Christian interfunction of theology and psychology.

Psychotheological Anthropology

The progress of the argument to this point suggests the usefulness of a summary evaluation of the current state of affairs in both psychological and theological anthropology. The space here permits the former, not the latter. The former is rampant with variety. The latter is largely confined to the highly speculative constructs of two philosophical traditions: a basically biblical theological perspective, largely scholastic or pietistic in shape, and a basically philosophical theological perspective, largely Tillichian in shape.

Psychological anthropology is most readily investigated through the plethora of personality theories developed in recent decades. One of the most definitive, and for me the most helpful, assessments of modern personality theories is that of Salvatore R. Maddi.[22]

Maddi's study treats the classic theorists from Freud to Fromm in terms of two primary categories; the manner in which each theory illumines matters regarding the core of human personality and matters regarding the periphery of human personality. Within those two categories of core and periphery, he describes each theory in terms of its essence as a conflict model or a fulfillment model of personality. He presents his own model, which he calls the consistency model, and then critiques each in terms of rational, empirical criteria applicable to both of the primary categories, core and periphery. Maddi defines personality as a

stable set of characteristics and tendencies that determine those commonalities and differences in the psychological behavior (thoughts, feelings, and actions) of people that have continuity in time and that may not be easily understood as the sole result of the social and biological pressures of the moment. Tendencies are the processes that determine directionality of thought, feelings, and actions. They are in the service of goals or functions. Characteristics are static or structural entities, usually implied by tendencies, that are used to explain not the movement toward goals or the achievement of function but rather the fact and content of goals or requirements.[23]

So human personality is a concept used to describe the observed phenomena that indicate the kind of person a given individual is, as indicated by his or her type response to life situations. The interpretation, of course, implies a perspective determined by one's essential assumptions regarding the nature of humanness. The anthropology operating is that concept of human nature functioning or forming in the interplay of those assumptions (speculation) and the observed phenomena (data).

Core attributes of human personality are those features common to all people that disclose the inherent attributes of human beings. Periphery facets of human personality, according to Maddi, are learned, not inherent, concrete, and close to the behavior itself, which can be observed.

Concerning the conflict, fulfillment, and consistency models, Maddi makes the following points. The conflict model assumes that human personality is the product of two great opposing and unchangeable forces, functioning at the psychosocial level or the intrapsychic level, between which forces the person is achieving a dynamic balance or a denial of either or both. The fulfillment model assumes only one force, localized in the person, and moving toward either actualization or perfection. The consistency model assumes no great dynamic forces at all, but rather a dynamic growth process of interaction with, and feedback from, the environment. "If the feedback is consistent with what was expected, or with what has been customary, there is quiescence. But if there is inconsistency between the feedback and the expectation or custom, there is pressure to decrease this uncomfortable state of affairs. Life is understood as the extended attempt to maintain consistence."[24]

Freud and Murray are cited as examples of the conflict model, psychosocial version; Rank, Jung, Perls, and others, examples of the conflict model, intrapsychic version. Rogers and Maslow illustrate for Maddi the fulfillment model, actualization version; Adler, White, Allport, Fromm, and Ellis, the fulfillment model, perfection version. The consistency model, cognitive dissonance version includes the early work of Kelly, McClelland, and Festinger; the consistency model, activation version, that of Fiske and Maddi.

It is precisely within the personality theory prevailing in each anthropological concept forming or functioning within each locus that the sciences of psychology and theology intersect. The critical issue here is the need to ferret out the anthropological assumptions and consequences of each of these personality theory views, and to determine how, in the interplay between the assumptions and the data, the psychotheological anthropology is being shaped. This is crucial for determining how one may responsibly bring a grace theology—formulated as the principles and perspectives of a tentative biblical anthropology—to bear on the interpretation of the observed behavioral data, and for fostering a soundly mature theological and psychological anthropology and personality theory (cf. fig. 10).

Conclusion

What can be asserted first, it seems to me, is that neither the biblical assumptions nor the empirical or psychological data has a higher warrant as truth or a higher logical, psychological, or theological valence than the other. Both must vitally participate in the interface of assumptions and data, for a mature anthropology and psychology theory to evolve.

Second, it is the contention of this chapter that the assumptions of the God-compatriot model of human status and the God-imager model of human nature, cast in terms of the evident fallenness of humans and also in terms of the radical, unconditional, and universal nature of God's covenant grace, are absolutely crucial assumptions to bring to bear upon the data, with a view to achieving an authentic psychotheological theory development process, not only in the area of personality theory development, but in all other areas of psychology theory development as well.

Third, a sound theory must be operational, in the sense that it provides adequate tools for the handling of concept definition and the associated concept measurement necessary to manage authentically the full range of data. A sound theory also must be precise, in that it must deal with the data pertinent to the specified problem or concern. Futhermore, it must be empirically, philosophically, and psychologically valid, in the sense that it manages the full range of data from all sources: empirical data, philosophical theological assumptions, and psychological perceptions.

Fourth, psychotheology theory development is crucial at each level of the intersection of psychology and theology: conceptual theoretical, research methodology, data base, and clinical experience.

Figure 10

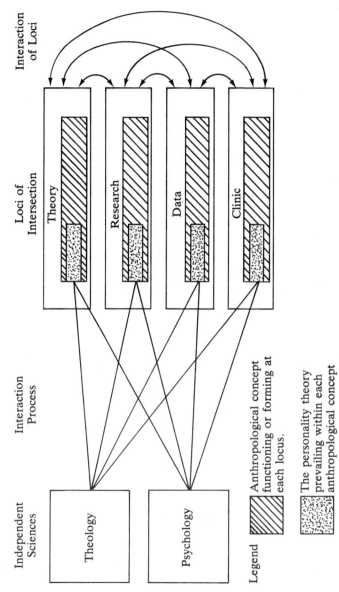

Fifth, the wide variety of personality theories—viewed as Maddi sees them or in the Hall-Lindzey categories of psychoanalytic, analytic, psychological, personological, field, individual, organismic, factor, S-R, operant reinforcement, self, existential, or personality theories—really come down to four types: rational, emotional, relational, and biological theories. For example, one might place Ellis in the first, Maslow and Rogers in the second, Perls and Erhard in the third, and Skinner in the fourth.

If one assumes humans to be essentially rational, that affects one's theory of education and healing, because it affects one's psychotheology of immaturity and illness. It suggests that illness is a deficit of appropriate information or coherence, as is immaturity. Education and healing require information and insight. If one assumes humans to be essentially emotional in nature, education and healing require sensitivity and freedom; immaturity and illness are from blocked emotionality. Relationality, as a model of how persons are, assumes the need for confrontation and interaction as states in which persons realize their person-hood. The biological definition of human nature assumes that illness or immaturity is the result of inappropriate stimuli producing a pathological state of response. So both healing and education require introduction of proper S-R process.

When one applies such categories as these, the crucial role one's anthropology plays in one's psychology theory development is readily evident. One can see how real the essentially religious nature of scientific theory development is, and how crucial a difference is made in sound psychology theory development by the enrollment of a Yahwist anthropology into the interaction of theological assumptions and data and of psychological assumptions and data.

Sixth, at the very least, sound biblical anthropology will disclose the fact that each of the four types of personality theory indicated above contains theologically valid elements:

rational, emotional, relational, and biological. A full-fledged Christian theory requires adequate comprehension of all these elements. Likewise, though a Yahwist biblical theology seems to me to militate in favor of Maddi's fulfillment model, actualization version, with such representatives as Rogers and Maslow, it must be said that, were one to adopt Maddi's categories completely, a sound biblical anthropology would disclose crucial truth in each of them.

Seventh, if a sound psychotheological anthropology is crucial to personality theory development, it will be crucial, as well, to the development of a theory of illness, a theory of wholeness, and a theory of healing. I propose to explore those matters in the next chapter.

In sum, therefore, I see theology and psychology as different perspectives or frames of reference, with differing fields of discourse, dealing with the same subject matter in our area of concern. Allport emphasized the importance of translating insights and concepts from each science to the other. They interact at four levels in the quest for truth about their subject: at the theoretical level of assumptions and concept and theory definition, at the research methodology level, at the data base level (what data to look for, how, description of the data), and at the clinical experience level. Their common subject is humanness. They intersect, therefore, in the anthropology that is functioning or forming at each level of intersection. The function and formation of anthropology at each level must continually form and inform the anthropology that functions and forms at all the other levels. Thus may the total range of potential insight in this quest for the truth about psychology and theology shape our mature anthropology, and thus may psychology and theology totally form and inform each other. Then McLemore may well prove correct in speaking of psychotheology as the Christian enterprise in the helping professions.

CHAPTER 6

Consequences for Psychotherapy

Introduction

Johann von Goethe observed that everybody wants to be somebody, but nobody wants to grow. That is not a universally applicable principle, fortunately, but it is what the therapist is often up against at the clinical level. That is, healing, education, maturation, and redemption are each a growth process, and there is a profound sense in which illness, ignorance, immaturity, and paganism are states or postures produced by obstruction of the needed growth. Likewise, the ultimate states of wholeness, wisdom and knowledge, maturity and wholesomeness, and salvation are the final integrated achievements to which growth brings us.

The process of growth hinges upon insight and the application of insight with regard to the state of our illness or need and with regard to the possibilities and methods for growing or inciting growth. This principle is true and generalized, whether the obstruction to growth experienced in a given person is psychological, physiological, intellectual, theological, or a combination of these.

I contend for that principle against the backdrop of a

Christian anthropology, structured by a Yahwist theology of grace: unconditional, radical, and universal. That is, I am assuming that God has imputed an inviolable status to humans, that the status is God-compatriot, means a role and status that is more than merely servant or son or daughter of God. It is a status and role of being, among other things, co-laborer with God in the "garden" Kingdom, a companion of God in the communion idealized by Adam's walks with God in the cool of the evening, and an imager of God's essential qualities and characteristics of communication, creativity, generativity, memory, self-conceptualization or self-consciousness, decisiveness, power, self-actualization, love, and the like. This assumption, moreover, includes the perception that not even God will abrogate that status, and that therefore he cannot.

This Christian anthropology implies that the nature of humans is being shaped by a discernable spectrum of magnificent potentials for psychological, physical, intellectual, and spiritual growth, and these, in turn, have remarkable potential for technological, scientific, cultural, and religious growth. This Christian anthropology further conceives the destiny of humans as the achievement of wholeness and integration through total actualization of the potentials inherent in humanness, i.e., inherent in the status of God-compatriot and God-imager.

A Psychotheology of Health

Thus, I maintain that, viewed psychologically or theologically, a complete understanding of humans centers in the dimension of anthropology having to do with the "chief end of man," i.e., the destiny to which we are coming, by the grace of Yahweh. Christian anthropology is teleological in orientation. Viewed in the psychological or theological frame of reference, wholeness can be seen as the state of ultimate teleological achievement and fulfillment through growth.

117

That may well be true of the cosmos as well. In that case, health is the state of having achieved wholeness or being in the process of achieving it and having achieved that degree appropriate to one's stage at any given time.

Christian psychologists, theologians, and clinicians, therefore, must begin to develop clinical criteria for assessing the process and a person's stage in it. Secular psychology, insofar as it represents unimpeachable truth regarding that level of the process it has investigated, provides Christians with much ready-made equipment for this endeavor. That secular equipment must be received gratefully and seriously, as a gift from God's revelation, and then employed in a psychotheological framework.

The principles for wholeness and health stated above, apply equally to physiological, psychological, intellectual, and spiritual spheres. They are equally true with regard to sickness of body, mind, and spirit, and apply as much to clinical pathology as to sinfulness and religious disorder.

A Psychotheology of Illness

If sound argumentation obtains so far, then it is possible for us to undertake a crucial task the Christian community has never succeeded in doing very well: describe a psychotheology of illness. In general, the subconscious posture of persons in Western culture, healing professionals and laypersons alike, with regard to those who are ill is surprisingly negative and stereotyped. The attitude of our culture is often that they are sick because they did not exercise enough, diet effectively, eat well enough, protect themselves properly, live well, stay youthful, or choose good genetic progenitors. We spontaneously assume that they are ill because God, fate, aging, destiny, or their misbehavior has finally caught up with them. We must admit that the ill are seen as second-class citizens. They are exploited, objectified, warehoused, manipulated, and generally handled as many preachers handle sinners.

Something in us arrogantly infers that the ill are getting what is coming to them, though we may empathize or sympathize.

That psychotheology of illness will not square with our Christian anthropology and the theology of grace. A sound psychotheology of illness must operate from the perspective that ill persons are God-compatriots of infinitely and inviolably worthy status, whose growth toward their divinely destined self-actualization at the physical, psychological, intellectual, or spiritual level has been obstructed. That state of obstruction and the loss of growth appropriate to the person's current level of expected development is by definition illness.

Sometimes the obstruction is a genetic distortion, a foreign organism, an imbalance of nutrition, a misfunction of metabolism, a disrupted socialization, a failure of appropriate instruction and guidance, inappropriate fear, ineffective worship, unchanneled assertiveness, or the like. Whatever it is, insight in the patient or applied by the healer is necessary to free the growth to health and wholeness once again. Sickness is not a state that implies moral import, but an existential state of affairs concerning which the only moral issue is whether the healer and the patient promote healing if and where it is potentially available.

A Psychotheology of Healing

It is predictable, then, that a psychotheology of healing deals with the method and substance in the enterprise of reducing the obstructions to growth and enhancing growth's vitality. This is the immediate level of concern to the clinician. It is imperative that the clinician's model of humanness is comprehensively shaped by a dynamic Christian anthropology, structured in terms of a thoroughgoing theology of grace, so that his or her psychotheology of illness, healing, and health or wholeness is a sound one. Moreover, the clinician's Christian anthropology, as that of the Christian scientist at the data base level, research methodology level, and theoretical level, must be dynamic, not static or dogmatic. It must be interacting constantly with his real clinical experience as well as with the work of his counterparts at the theoretical, research, and data levels, so that the clinician's Christian anthropology is constantly being reshaped and refined by the combined experience of all four levels of the quest, and thus progressively maturing.

Models of Psychopathology and Psychotherapy

In 1974 Siegler and Osmond provided some interesting comparative insights and some useful focus to the field of clinical psychology.[1] In their book *Models of Madness, Models of Medicine,* they presented a table of the eight major current models of psychopathology. For each model they described twelve typical clinical functions, including diagnosis or definition, etiology, subject behavior, treatment, prognosis, therapy setting, types of therapists, rights of the patient and of the patient's social unit, and goals of therapy.

Siegler and Osmond describe the current models with their definitions of psychopathology. The *medical model* assumes a physician will diagnose the illness, rule out others, inform the patient, and determine treatment and prognosis. Natural causes are assumed to be the sources of the disorder. The goal of the process is to prevent worsened illness, to cure the symptoms and, if possible, the source, and to accumulate medical knowledge. The *moral model* assumes that a moral practitioner will determine the nature and extent of the disfunction or inappropriate, and hence immoral, behavior. The etiology is assumed to be unimportant but is learned bad behavior. Treatment modifies bad behavior with discipline: positive and negative sanctions. Prognosis is considered good if the patient cooperates in the establishing of functional sanction systems and reinforcement schedules. The goal of therapy is to alter the patient's behavior with acceptable social norms.

The *impaired model* sees the patient as permanently maimed and is unconcerned with most of the twelve functions, except diagnosis and institutionalization. The goal is to protect the patient from society and vice versa. Anything short of permanent impairment is not identified as clinical pathology. The *psychoanalytic model* assumes patients are somewhere on a continuum from mild neurosis to severe psychosis. Diagnosis is not significant; etiology is very important; therapy involves decoding the patient's symbolic systems and creating the transference base, enhancing the patient's move toward health. The patient has the right to sympathy, empathy, and progress toward health. The goal is to resolve the pathogenic conflicts, intrapsychic or psycho-social in nature.

The *social model* assumes that society is sick and the patient's pathology is accidental to that. The sociopathology of the patient can be corrected by social change in the community. The rights and goals of society, the patient, and the therapist focus on creation of a healthy social environment for growth, especially of children. The *psychedelic model* sees psychopathology as a mind-expanding trip prompted by families or communities who drive patients crazy. Therapy involves breaking the family bond, providing a "guided trip" to enlightenment, and so allowing the patient to develop the inner potential to change self and world.

The *conspirational model* assumes that pathology is a label given to the patient by others who cannot tolerate deviance. Treatment is brainwashing for the purpose of maintaining the status quo. The *family interactional model* assumes that patients are the index of family pathology. The patient's symptoms are an enactment of the family's pathology. Family therapy is required and, if effective, the family will give up its pathological game pattern and the index person can drop the personal symptoms. The goal of therapy is to understand the family dynamics and restore pathological families to functional relationships.

It is evident that each of the models described comprehends some aspect of the truth with which clinicians must deal. It is interesting that the theorist who has come closest to devising a psychotheology of illness and therapy, Jay Adams, falls into the moral model, which is the least reflective of the full range of data available and the farthest from sound psychology and a Christian anthropology rooted in a thoroughgoing theology of grace, in the biblical tradition of the Yahwist.

It is impossible here to critique each of the Sieglar-Osmond categories in detail, but a few observations may be useful. First, the social model, though it embodies some reality, has thoroughly disfunctioned in our society, as indicated by the hopeless ineffectiveness of the costly strategies for basic social change attempted over forty years from the individual and local level to the federal government level. It is indicated further by the recent acknowledgment that the longstanding ambition for criminal rehabilitation has not worked and is scientifically and culturally bankrupt. The impaired model, psychedelic model, and conspirational model offer no comprehensive usefulness at all. The medical model and family interaction models are much more comprehensively applicable, but both are deficient in their assessment of the seriousness of the general patient's depth and degree of disorder. The psychoanalytic model comes closest to appreciating the radical extent and depth of human pathology, but like the medical and family models, it fails to appreciate adequately the pathological state of human beings generally, the radical depth of our alienation, from our real potentials and our destiny. It fails, therefore, to appreciate the real dimension of generalized pathogenic anxiety and dissonance, intrapsychic and psychosocial, which lie at the root of human pathology and are inherent in the current state of humanness.

The self-perceived fallenness, alienation, and isolation at the core of our humanness is underestimated.

A Christian Clinical Approach

A Christian psychotheological model of pathology and therapy is essential. It must incorporate an adequate appreciation of our real sense of universal human lostness, expressive of the distance between our destiny and our daily function, between our potentials and our problematic state of underachievement, between our imagination and our performance, between our reach and our grasp. It must appreciate the physical stress and distress, the psychopathogenesis, and the spiritual defeat reflected in and generated by that distance between God's realities for us and our own realities in us.

In the previous chapter, I noted that in developing psychological theory, the history of personality theory could be categorized in four different models: those theories assuming human personality to be essentially rational, emotional, relational, or biological. A brief discussion of these four models is relevant to the development of a sound Christian clinical perspective.

If one assumes, as Socrates did and A. Ellis does, that human nature or personality is essentially rational, then pathology is the lack or loss of "the well-considered life." This suggests that intellectual wholeness comes by information through education. Psychological wholeness then comes by insight through informative therapy, being led to think rightly. Spiritual wholeness is then dependent upon comprehension of the wisdom of God in Christ, generally considered to be dogmatic in form. The lack of insight and information at any of these levels produces pathology in that category of human function affected by the lack, according to rational types of personality theory.

If one assumes that human nature is essentially emotional,

123

as Maslow and Rogers do, then true humanness is achieved in authentic emotionality. Implied in this set of personality theories is the notion that pathology is the obstruction or lack of authenticity and of freedom of the emotional fields or emotional world of the person. This does not imply that emotions are always arbitrarily productive or affirmable or that it is always more healthy to act on any or all emotions at any or all times. It implies rather that the potential to do so and the freedom to decide about that is crucial to authentic humanness and health.

In this model, intellectual health is achieved by freeing the emotive world through training to offer its truth and reality to the cognitive perception of things. Psychological health requires the emotional freedom that eliminates intrapsychic dissonance or confliction. This will lead to psychosocial adjustment, coping, and health. The lack of that freedom is pathology.

The relational model assumes that persons achieve selfhood only in relationality. This is different than saying good emotional or rational relationships produce health. It is rather the assertion that we are an authentic self only while interacting. Gestalt and EST might be cited as cases in point. Pathology results from the fear or lack of opportunity to interact, to confront and assert one's self over against another. Health at each level is the function of actual encounter and the change it induces in the state of being of the person while encountering. Some residual effect is assumed, but it is not valued except as it is realized in the next encounter.

The biological model with its Skinnerian determinism assumes that pathology is the breakdown of response to stimuli, and health is the restoration of efficient S-R process and dynamic. Behaviorism provides useful insights, but it seems to me that its real value is grossly disproportionate to its current popularity and press.

Christian clinicians need to use the insights from all four

categories in building a clinically functional Christian anthropology and psychotheology. However, the one that lends itself most readily to the clinical perspective rooted in a thoroughgoing theology of grace is the emotional model. It takes the entire question of the human spirit, human nature as a divine imager, human potential and self-actualization, and the fragile human longing for a gracelike, unconditional personal regard, most seriously, at least in potential. Rogers' notions of the inviolable integrity of the person and personality of the patient at the point where he or she is, at any given therapeutic moment or event, his process model of psychotherapy, and his concept of the fully functioning person as the goal of therapy and of life provide a useful framework that lends itself readily to the grace-oriented clinical perspective. That is amenable to embracing the function of a Hebrew type of perception of truth and reality while valuing no less the historic Western emphasis on the Greek type of scientific methodology.

The development of a Christian therapeutic strategy that adequately reflects the kind of Christian anthropology that is implied in a thoroughgoing grace theology will include the following applied characteristics. First, the incarnation in the therapist of the unconditional acceptance of the patient, where the patient is at the moment in his or her pathology.

Second, a profound empathy that places the therapist inside the psychological frame of reference in which the patient experiences the pathology. This will lead to the therapist's endeavor to determine the sources and nature of the obstructions to health as well as the possibilities, in and for the patient, for reinitiating growth. This empathic incarnation of God's grace empowers the therapist to affirm the patient as a person, not just as patient, as God has affirmed us in taking us and our alienation so seriously as to visit us in his son. Such verbal and nonverbal mediation of God's unconditional acceptance of persons, including the patient, is a crucial base line for the patient's recovery of a perception of self-worth, power, and destiny that rings true to his or her real nature as a potentially whole person, fulfilled in all the possibilities that the arbitrarily imputed status of God-compatriot and the nature of God-imager implies.

Third, the Christian therapist will provide the patient with a sense of the mutuality of the quest for wholeness for the patient, upon which the patient-therapist team has embarked.

Fourth, it will be made evident in the therapy process that the therapist, too, is wrestling with his or her own humanness, with both its pathology and its potential.

Fifth, it will become evident in a sound Christian therapeutic strategy that the therapist's world view expresses a comprehensive ambition for the wholeness of the whole world of humans and things and that the patient's wholeness is quested for in that setting.

Sixth, the possibilities and expectations for the patient's wholeness inherent in that world view will become apparent.

Seventh, the grace imputed status of the patient as compatriot of God will become evident to the patient, as the underpinning reality of the world view.

Eighth, soundly established techniques for countering defensive patterns in the patient will be utilized to defeat any obstruction of growth to wholeness.

Ninth, the patient's physical, intellectual, psychological, and spiritual needs and states will be taken seriously as functions of a whole-person concern for wholeness and wholesomeness.

Tenth, the effectiveness of therapy will be measured in relative terms at each level of increased functionality—physical, psychological, intellectual, and spiritual—in the light of the expectation that the ultimate achievement of health will be the arrival at spiritual, as well as psychological, maturity.

Some Christian professionals recently active especially in the pastoral care movements, such as Thomas C. Oden, have severely denigrated the clinical perspective and psycho-theological model of healing. They are reverting to what Wayne Oates has called a pseudo-classical style of pastoral counseling. Oden's recent article in the *Military Chaplains Review,* e.g., seems to suggest a new stage of evangelicalism in his thought, but his conceptualization of healing or therapy is moralistic.[2] He has reverted to a somewhat primitive and antipsychology notion, it appears. That kind of forced attempt to relate Christian faith and the healing enterprise at the applied level will be of no service to the Christian concern and dialogue for an authentic psychotheology. It is, rather, a return to a directive form of ecclesiasticism in the helping professions that, like Jay Adams' similar devices of moraliza-tion and conditional grace, rather than provide a classic new model of Christian healing, will undermine the hard-won progress of the last decades. That regression is to be assiduously avoided. Both psychology and theology have managed too well and come too far to warrant an anticlinical and antigrace-theology iconoclasm at this point.

Clinical Consequences for Psychotherapy

The consequences for psychotherapy of a thoroughgoing grace theology and the Christian anthropology inherent in it might be elaborated at great length. I have done that in other pulications. Here I shall merely summarize the more obviously relevant ones.

To operate clinically from the perspective that humans image God and are imputed an inviolable status of God-compatriot leads the therapist to an appreciation of human persons as of infinite worth, dignity, and esteem and as possessing a preestablished identity to be fully realized through growth, in spite of themselves, untrammeled by their illness.

Second, it urges upon the therapist the principle that the

root of pathology is alienation, requiring eclipse by a God-like acceptance of the patient by the therapist.

Third, it urges that the acceptance is unconditional.

Fourth, it urges that sin is more precisely a failure of destiny than a failure of duty.

Fifth, the goal of therapy and the view of the possibilities of wholeness in the patient are greatly clarified by the perspective urged.

Sixth, the above insights will work toward defusing neurotic guilt, anxiety, remorse, hopelessness, grief, self-pity, low self-esteem, and compulsivity and will restore a sense of inherent dignity and freedom in the patient.

Seventh, this clinical model is likely to remove the panic of the therapist regarding the awesome clinical responsibility to bring health to the patient. This frees the therapist to make the God-like decisions often necessary in therapeutic process. This clinical model should also effect meaningful, constructive anxiety reduction for the patient who perceives that he or she does not need to get well in order to be accepted and cherished, certified and honored, by the therapist and by God. And thus the patient is free to get well in a naturally unfolding, unpanicked growth process. The patient will be led to recognize that his or her worthiness is inherent, not earned by measuring up to the therapist's expectations, his or her own, or God's.

Eighth, this clinical model provides a setting of trust, transference, and increased potential for the risk taking necessary to growth and of reduced injection of therapist pathology into the growth frame of the patient.

Ninth, this clinical perspective frees the therapist and patient to be usefully humorous about themselves, each other, and their pathologies and potentials.

Tenth, this model enhances the patient's self-acceptance as a mortal person, a dying person in a generation of dying persons, but secured and cherished redemptively and eternally in the hand of Yahweh.

For me, the Christian enterprise of healing people holds out one additional and overriding dimension: the incomparable encouragement and delight that, though I may never see patients again, in their need and quandary, I shall with certainty celebrate with them and all the saints of God our mutual ecstasy of gratitude one great and glorious morning when faith has become sight, when we shall see reality whole and face-to-face, and know and affirm God as thoroughly as God now knows and affirms us.

CHAPTER 7

Concluding Observations: Transference and the Christian Therapist

The sources of the psychological sciences spring from antiquity.[1] The development of the art of psychotherapy depends significantly upon the early Christian church and its concern for and with the human psyche. That early practice, in a primitive way, integrated psychological process and Christian experience. For example, it must at least be said of the Roman Catholic confessional, seen in the light of Scripture and St. Augustine, that its value lay in the psychotherapeutic effects of reality confrontation, catharsis, anxiety resolution through acceptance, certification of self, and behavior modification.[2] Luther therefore favored preserving the confessional in Protestant practice.[3] Moreover, the long history of pastoral care was a primitive and moderately successful psychotherapeutic enterprise integrating psychological process and Christian experience. The church community's support systems, confession and certification systems, values clarification systems, identity and self-esteem clarification systems, and purpose and behavior-structuring systems are all forces for psychological healing, social certification, and spiritual reinforcement.[4] Unfortunately, those structures and processes frequently have been transformed into destructive forces, fostering negative valuing of persons, coercion, rejection patterns, pathogenic conformity and achievement demands, and reinforcements of self-defeating dependency. It consistently has been the heroic pastor and the specially inspirited local communities of the church that have succeeded in building the kind of communion of trust and base of transference that have made holistic ministry a reality.

The Christian Therapist and Transference

Transference is a priority concern in effective therapy. Without it little constructive movement can be expected. Negative transference inevitably structures the therapeutic process in detrimental ways. Positive transference establishes the base of trust in terms of which insight, affirmation, and growth become possible and resistance can be wholesomely eroded. Transference may be described as including the mutual affirmation of client and therapist while reserving affirmation from pathological behavior or feeling patterns in the client. This affirmation of the person qua person may be described from the client's posture as adoption of the therapist in a number of healthful or health neutral roles. The client may establish a useful transference, e.g., by adopting the therapist in the role of a parent, a friend, a confidant, a partner in the quest to health, a professional counselor, family member, or loved one. The therapist may establish a useful transference by accepting the client in a dependent role, client role, familial role, or loved one role. Normally, the process of transference moves through most of these roles during the progress of the therapeutic experience.

The essence of both positive transference and counter-transference is the mutual acceptance and certification of the personhood of the parties in therapy, making possible effective transference, with the trust and certification that effects, that is the essence of agape and of grace.[5] Whatever is effective in good transference in a given client's need situation will be and produce the Christian experience he or she most needs at the outset, i.e., acceptance of the person in need, apart from decisions regarding requirements for modification in attitude and behavior. Jung speaks of a kind of constructive projection essential to positive transference in which the client accords the therapist the aura of the archetype healer. Jung states that that projective process is as crucial to healing as the actual therapeutic strategy itself.[6]

Christian experience for client and Christian expression for therapist in positive and negative psychological processes depend exclusively on whether the psychological processes are managed toward genuine healing. Some guilt-ridden clients project a need to see the therapist as an authoritarian judge. Other neurotic clients need to experience confirmation of their neuroses by projecting rejection of client upon the therapist and his strategies. Still others need to ingratiate themselves with the therapist to prove their own self-worth or to create situations that seem to certify the client's perceived rejection by a therapist who declines the importunity.

There is a grave danger in the therapeutic process that the unlearned or unskilled therapist may be drawn inadvertently into these traps, thereby reinforcing the client's pathology, rather than healing. Supporting and confirming the client's pathology by therapeutic ineptness is the prime threat to authentic Christian experience in therapy, to the degree that the ineptness is unwholesome psychological process.

Similarly in circumstances in which a client accords the therapist a projected role of approval, acceptance, and certification of pathological behavior, when the therapist intended only acceptance and certification of the person qua person, unhealthful psychological process obstructs constructive Christian experience or growth.

Moreover, since therapists also may be pathological in

needs and relationships, obstructive psychological processes also may emanate from therapists. Projecting the client into a role necessary to fulfill the therapist's pathological or non-therapeutic needs, such as acceptance of counterproductive client dependency upon the therapist or acceptance of the client's ingratiating role, obstructs Christian growth in the manner and degree that it is psychologically counterproductive. A truly Christian caring therapist is repeatedly involved in transference and projection relationships in which the distinction between the wholesome Christian process of agape and the other potentially damaging psychological processes is difficult to keep clear. It is a simplistic denial process to rationalize such a predicament as a Platonic relationship. There are no Platonic relationships, i.e., nonsexual relationships. All relationships, wholesome or unwholesome, in therapy or out of it, are sexual in some significant dimension—we are all aware at any given moment of the maleness or femaleness of the person next to us.

On the other hand, certain forms of role identification, transference, and projection are apparently therapeutically and Christianly relevant. The therapist's perception of the "healer-healed" role relationship is soundly Jungian and Christian. Similarly, the therapist's perception of the client in parent-child roles or in a partnership role at certain stages of the therapy may be Christian insofar as it is productive of healing.

The Christian Therapist and Resistance

In a very general sense all psychoses, except those chemically induced, may be discussed as the result of subconscious "decisions" for escape from pain and the mystification of reality into a "sick world" projection. Moreover, inhibitions, denial, depressive response to unexpressible anger, ambivalence, unidentified or inappropriate anxiety, masking and excessive verbal stimulation are psychological processes that defend against the need to deal with internal and external reality. Hence they defend against health.

The Christian experience of the client and the Christian role of the therapist depend upon the willingness to risk pursuit of the client's psychological needs rather than "wants." Too often sympathy and sentimentality have been accepted by the Christian therapist as the agapic response to defensive pathologies. Sympathy and sentiment are not distinctively Christian expressions and can never substitute for genuine psychological empathy and the confrontation of client defensive strategies. Love is usually tough stuff. If these defensive strategies are sympathetically reinforced or approved, or are not critically confronted, health and growth, psychologically and spiritually, are impossible.

In sum, what is Christian in these matters is what works psychologically, since agape is the pursuit, at all cost, of what heals the needy human and enhances growth. Psychological growth and growth in Christian experience differ in specific ways, but they move toward the objective of the totally complete and fulfilled person. The specific differences have to do with technique and insight content and therefore may have differing therapeutic effects.

The Christian Therapist and Therapeutic Realism

Coping with realism as a Christian client or therapist requires acknowledgment of the crucial fact that Christian psychotherapy must be kept distinct from Christian moralization. Christian morals are crucial to total personality health and fulfillment, but the psychotherapeutic process is to be conditioned by the strategies that bring that health to this client in his or her current state of need, not by strategies designed to defend Christian moral structure as the primary objective.

Since agape is the Christian process of people-handling and since sympathy, sentimentalism, and moralization are escapes from exercising that love, the Christian therapist must insist that only good scientific psychology can become Christian therapy. Confrontation of and coping with reality in Christian psychotherapy requires those conditions in which the therapist's client-acceptance is of such a nature as to afford the client self-acceptance. That, in turn, will produce the conditions in which the client is empowered to accept the reality intrinsic and extrinsic to himself or herself in those terms necessary to homeostasis and appropriate change processes. There is a discernible interaction between experiencing God's unconditional acceptance, experiencing the therapist's transference acceptance, and experiencing the ability to accept and change oneself as client.

The Christian Therapist and Devotional Tools

Legitimate techniques for achieving the relief and discipline of the Christian's healthy experience of saying, "If God feels like that about me, I want to be his kind of guy," may include bibliotherapy in scriptural insights, "therapeutic instruction" in the pychotherapy process, fixing insight-achievement through client confession/affirmation of faith, and the like.

The danger of this process is that the Christian structures and affirmations become the primary process and that sound psychotherapeutic process becomes its assistant. That is generally counterproductive to psychotherapy. Moreover, the essential nature of an overwhelming percentage of psychopathologies, which distort and confuse, especially sexual and spiritual disorders, is such that a psychotherapeutic technique that is primarily "Christian guidance" or that plays into the client's religio-psychic disorders will reinforce, not heal, the disorder.

When a patient has achieved some healthful level of realism and self-acceptance, development of some wholesome disciplines of the Christian world view and life may be possible, together with progress to a Christ-appropriate social and religious process. Presumably such a pattern of Christian perception, perspective, and function would include all levels of personality function: social, psychological, religious, and spiritual—a life of trust vs. fear, self-acceptance vs. perfectionism, and self-forgiveness (humility) vs. self-righteousness. That Christian way of life will also produce health manifestations such as (a) prayer, worship, and liturgy experienced as grace-celebration, not God-manipulation; (b) rationality vs. mysticism and charism; (c) humanness vs.supernaturalism; and therefore, (d) "incarnation theology" vs."divine invasion" theology.

Healthy persons and healthy Christian persons, in short, are those who have achieved sufficient integrity, useful contact with the reality of their feeling world, sufficient awareness of the tentativeness of all human perception, a growth, rather than a static, "arrival" perspective regarding self and others, a certainty of God's grace in Christ, and a celebration of the Christian way, which is epitomized in Scripture and which leads to authenticity.[7]

It is difficult to assess how directive a therapist can afford to be regarding the use of prayer, worship, confession of sin, or of faith in all this. Surely the Christian therapist will feel an authentic need for treating the client holistically to a complete sense of meaning, motivation, and appropriate Christian behavior. Such growth is completed in Christ and his way. However, suggestions for achieving that completion may go beyond the necessities of functional psychological health. Then, perhaps they should be dealt with as a stage of care beyond psychotherapy. That Christian caring is appropriate to a therapist-client relation, even if in a specific case it is not appropriate to the therapy process itself. The role of an effective church congregation as a support-community often proves most helpful in this regard.

The question remains as to whether prayer, worship, liturgical behavior, biblical instruction, encouragement to conversion, or stressing sanctification is necessary, useful, or permissible in therapy or as part of therapy. Such technique is dangerous, not because it lacks affinity to scientific enterprise of psychology or the discrete area of psychotherapy, but because these religious phenomena so readily play into the pathology of the client or of the therapist. That does not mean that these techniques should be proscribed. It means that they should be used only in a setting where a therapist has satisfactorily established that there are no pathologies into which such spiritual emphases or religious activities will play pathologically.[8] The Christian way for a Christian therapist to treat a Christian client whose religious practices are of such a distorted nature or effect as to reinforce or even create his pathological disfunction is to urge him to eliminate those religious procedures. The new creature in Christ is intended to be at least healthy and whole in his psyche, even if not unusually religious. Psychological health and Christian life require at least spiritual freedom, even if the processes of Christian life and discipline may not be mature and complete.

Notes

Preface

1. J. F. Williams, *Personal Hygiene Applied,* 8th ed. (Philadelphia: W. B. Saunders Co., 1946), p. 2.

Chapter 1

1. See also J. Harold Ellens, "Psychological Dynamics in Christian Worship: A Beginning Inquiry," *Journal of Psychology and Theology,* 1:4 (October 1973): 10-19.

2. Karen Horney, *Neurotic Personality of Our Time* (New York: W. W. Norton & Co., 1937), pp. 41-42.

3. Ibid., pp. 43-44.

4. Ibid., p. 47.

5. Ibid., p. 48.

6. In Seward Hiltner and Karl Menninger, *Constructive Aspects of Anxiety* (Nashville: Abingdon, 1963), pp. 93-95.

7. Barbara Mertz, *Red Land, Black Land* (New York: Coward, McCann & Geoghegan, 1966), p. 367.

8. See also Edward J. Carnell, *The Burden of Søren Kierkegaard* (Grand Rapids: Eerdmans Publishing Co., 1965).

9. M. Eliade, *Yoga: Immortality and Freedom* (New York: Pantheon Books, 1958), p. xix.

10. In J. G. Arapura, *Religion as Anxiety and Tranquility* (Paris: Mouton, 1973), p. 53.

11. Ibid., p. 80.

12. Horney, p. 47.

13. Rollo May, *Meaning of Anxiety* (New York: Ronald Press, 1950). See the analysis of anxiety as loss of worthwhileness in the writings of Wolfe, Auden, Camus, Kafka, and Hesse (pp. 4-8). See also the section on the philosophy of religion.

14. Paul Tillich, *The Protestant Era* (Chicago: University of Chicago Press, 1948), p. 147.

Chapter 2

1. Peter Ellis, *The Yahwist: The Bible's First Theologian* (Notre Dame, Ind.: Fides Publishers, 1968).

2. Brevard S. Childs, *Introduction to the Old Testament as Scripture* (Philadelphia: Fortress Press, 1979).

3. Barbara Mertz, *Red Land, Black Land* (New York: Coward, McCann & Geoghegan, 1966).

4. Eric Fromm, *The Anatomy of Human Destructiveness* (New York: Holt, Rinehart and Winston, 1973).

5. John G. Finch, *The Message of Anxiety*. Taped lecture, CAPS-WACPS Convention, 1976.

6. Seward Hiltner and Karl Menninger, eds., *Constructive Aspects of Anxiety* (Nashville: Abingdon Press, 1963).

7. Rollo May, *Love and Will* (New York: W. W. Norton & Co., 1969).

8. C. Markham Berry, "Entering Canaan: Adolescence as a Stage of Spiritual Growth," *The Bulletin* of CAPS 6:4 (1980).

9. David J. A. Clines, "The Image of God in Man," *Tyndale Bulletin* 19 (1968): 53. Cf. also pp. 60, 87-90, 94-95, 97-99.

10. J. Christiaan Beker, *Paul the Apostle: The Triumph of God in Life and Thought* (Philadelphia: Fortress Press, 1980).

11. James Daane, *The Freedom of God* (Grand Rapids: Eerdmans Publishing Co., 1973).

12. Neil Punt, *Unconditional Good News: Toward an Understanding of Biblical Universalism* (Grand Rapids: Eerdmans Publishing Co., 1980).

Chapter 5

1. Nicholas Wolterstorff, *Reason Within the Bounds of Religion* (Grand Rapids: Eerdmans Publishing Co., 1976).

2. Egbert Schuurman, *Technology and the Future: A Philosophical Challenge* (New York: Radix Books, 1980). See also Donald MacKay, *The Clock Work Image: A Christian Perspective on Science* (Downers Grove, Ill.: Inter-Varsity Press, 1974) and Clifton J. Orlebeke, "Donald MacKay's Philosophy of Science," *Christian Scholars Review* 7:1 (1977).

3. Egbert Schuurman, *Reflections of the Technological Society* (Toronto: Wedge, 1980).

4. University of Chicago Press, 1978.

5. University of Chicago Press, forthcoming.

6. "Christian Counseling: Issues and Trends," *The Bulletin* of CAPS 6:4 (1980): 1.

7. *JPT* 2:2 (Spring 1974): 116.

8. Francis A. Schaeffer, *Escape from Reason* (Downers Grove, Ill.: Inter-Varsity Press, 1968); *True Spirituality* (Wheaton: Tyndale House, 1971).

9. J. H. Ellens, "Biblical Themes in Psychological Theory and Practice," *The Bulletin* of CAPS 6:2 (1980).

10. Francis A. Schaeffer, *Genesis in Space and Time* (Downers Grove, Ill.: Inter-Varsity Press, 1972), p. 165. Richard H. Bube, "Toward a Christian View of Science," *Journal of the American Scientific Affiliation* 32:4 (1971) and *The Human Quest* (Waco, Tex.: Word Books, 1976).

11. *JPT* 4:3 (Summer 1976).

12. Paul W. Clement and Niel C. Warren, "Can Religion and Psychotherapy Be Happily Married?" in *Religious Systems and Psychotherapy,* Ed. R. H. Cox (Springfield: Thomas, 1973).

13. Kenneth Mathisen, "Back to Basics: A Broad Conceptual Model for the Integration of Psychology and Theology," *JPT* 8:3 (Fall 1980): 222 ff.

14. C. Markham Berry, "Approaching the Integration of the Social Sciences and Biblical Theology," *JPT* 8:1 (Spring 1980): 33.

15. Ronald L. Koteskey, "Reaction: Theory or Data," *JPT* 8:3 (Fall 1980). Robert E. Larzelere, "The Task Ahead: Six Levels of Integration of Christianity and Psychology," *JPT* 8:1 (Spring 1980): 3. Gary Collins, *The Rebuilding of Psychology* (Wheaton: Tyndale House, 1977).

16. J. Roland Fleck and John D. Carter, *Psychology and Christianity: Integrative Readings* (Nashville: Abingdon, 1981).

17. Arnold H. De Graaf, "Toward an Integral Model of Psychotherapy," *The Bulletin* of CAPS 6:3 (1980): 7.

18. Jack Boghasian, "Theology Recapitulates Ontogeny: Reality Testing as an Analogy in Relating to God," *JPT* 8:2 (Summer 1980): 122.

19. New York: W. W. Norton & Co., 1960.

20. J. Harold Ellens, "Concepts of Self in Christian Experience and Psychotherapy," "Humanization of Man in the Antique World," and "Concepts of the Self in Biblical Theology." A series of lectures delivered at the Society of Biblical Literature and Exegesis, 1979.

21. It would be intriguing to explore, at this juncture, the relative role of right brain dominance and left brain dominance of the Eastern and Western churches' approaches and the Augustinian and Aristotelian approaches, respectively. See also Richard M. Restak, *The Brain: The Last Frontier* (Garden City, N. Y.: Doubleday & Co., 1979).

22. Salvatore R. Maddi, ed. *Personality Theories: A Comparative Analysis,* 4th ed. (Homewood, Ill.: The Dorsey Press, 1980).

23. Ibid., p. 10.

24. Ibid., p. 24.

Chapter 6

1. Miriam Siegler and Humphrey Osmond, *Models of Madness, Models of Medicine* (New York: The Macmillan Co., 1974).
2. Fall 1980.

Chapter 7

1. Aristotle, *Rhetoric* and *Poetics* (New York: Modern Library, 1955). Cf. also Hippocrates and Galen.
2. St. Augustine, *Confessions* (New York: E. P. Dutton, 1950). See also C. W. Brister, *Pastoral Care in the Church* (New York: Harper & Row, 1964), pp. 167-99 and W. A. Clebsch and C. R. Jaekle, *Pastoral Care in Historical Perspective* (New York: Jason Aronson, Inc., [1964] 1975), pp 13-23.
3. Martin Luther, *Works,* vol. 12 (St. Louis: Concordia Publishing House, 1955).
4. Acts 2:36-47. See Leslie D. Weatherhead, *Psychology, Religion, and Healing* (Nashville: Abingdon, 1952), pp. 70-88. Cf. also Galatians 6 and James 5:13-20.
5. Smiley Blanton with Edward Robinson, *Love or Perish,* exp. ed. (New York: Simon & Schuster, 1957), pp. 192-272. See also Louis Linn and Leo Schwarz, *Psychiatry and Religious Experience* (New York: Random House, 1958), pp. 80-116.
6. Carl Jung, *Undiscovered Self,* trans. R. F. C. Hull (Boston: Little, Brown, 1958).
7. 1 Cor. 13, Rom. 8, 1 John 3:1-3. Paul E. Johnson, *Psychology of Religion,* rev. and enl. ed. (Nashville: Abingdon Press, 1959), pp. 230-51; Edward E. Thornton, *Theology and Pastoral Counseling* (Philadelphia: Fortress Press, 1967).
8. Earl H. Furgeson, "Mental Illness Masquerading in Religious Terms," N. S. Cryer, Jr. and J. M. Vayhinger, eds., *Casebook in Pastoral Counseling* (Nashville: Abingdon Press, 1962), pp. 196-98. See also Linn and Schwarz, *Psychiatry and Religious Experience,* pp. 195-211; Seward Hiltner, *Pastoral Counseling* (Nashville: Abingdon Press, 1949), pp. 187 ff. Cf. also Dr. J. Harold Ellens, "Communication Theory and Petitionary Prayer," *JPT* 5:1 (Winter 1977).

Bibliography

Allen, Reginald E., ed. *Greek Philosophy: Thales to Aristotle.* New York: Free Press-Macmillan, 1966.

Arapura, J. G. *Religion as Anxiety and Tranquility.* Paris: Mouton, 1973.

Beker, J. Christiaan. *Paul the Apostle: The Triumph of God in Life and Thought.* Philadelphia: Fortress Press, 1980.

Berry, C. Markham. "Approaching the Integration of the Social Sciences and Biblical Theology." *JPT* 8:1 (Spring 1980).

———. "Entering Canaan: Adolescence as a Stage of Spiritual Growth." *The Bulletin* of CAPS 6:4 (1980).

Blanton, Smiley, with Edward Robinson. *Love or Perish.* Exp. ed. New York: Simon & Schuster, 1957.

Boghasian, Jack. "Theology Recapitulates Ontogeny: Reality Testing as an Analogy in Relating to God." *JPT* 8:2 (Summer 1980).

Boman, Thorleif. *Hebrew Thought Compared with Greek.* Tr. by Jules L. Moreau. New York: W. W. Norton & Co., 1960.

Bratton, F. G. *Myths and Legends of the Ancient Near East.* New York: Thomas Y. Crowell, 1970.

Brister, C. W. *Pastoral Care in the Church.* New York: Harper & Row, 1964.

Bromiley, G. W. *Christian Ministry.* Grand Rapids: Eerdmans Publishing Co., 1960.

Bry, Adelaide. *The TA Primer.* New York: Harper & Row, 1973.

Bube, Richard H. "Toward a Christian View of Science." *JASA* 32:4 (1971).

———. *The Human Quest.* Waco, Tex.: Word Books, 1976.

Bufford, Rodger. "Christian Counseling: Issues and Trends." *The Bulletin* of CAPS 6:4 (1980).

Bulfinch, Thomas. *Bulfinch's Mythology.* Abr. ed. Ed. by Edmund Fuller. New York: Dell Books, 1959.

Burn, A. R. *The Pelican History of Greece.* Baltimore: Penguin Books, 1966.

Burnet. John. *Early Greek Philosophy.* New York: New American Library [Meridian], 1957.

Carter, John D., and Narramore, Bruce. *The Integration of Psychology and Theology: An Introduction.* Grand Rapids: Zondervan Publishing House, 1979.

Childs, Brevard S. *Introduction to the Old Testament as Scripture.* Philadelphia: Fortress Press, 1979.

Clebsch, William A., and Jaekle, Charles R. *Pastoral Care in Historical Perspective.* New York: Jason Aronson, Inc., [1947] 1975.

Clement, Paul W., and Warren, Niel C. "Can Religion and Psychotherapy Be Happily Married?" In *Religious Systems and Psychotherapy,* R. H. Cox, ed. Springfield: Thomas, 1973.

Clifford, P. R. *The Pastoral Calling.* New York: Channel, 1961.

Clinebell, Howard J. *Basic Types of Pastoral Counseling.* Nashville: Abingdon Press, 1966.

———. *Growth Counseling: Hope-Centered Methods of Actualizing Human Wholeness.* Nashville: Abingdon, 1979.

Clines, David J. A. "The Image of God in Man." *Tyndale Bulletin* 19 (1968).

Cochrane, Charles N. *Christianity and Classical Culture: A Study of Thought and Action from Augustus to Augustine.* New York: Oxford University Press, 1957.

Collins, Gary. *The Rebuilding of Psychology.* Wheaton: Tyndale House, 1977.

Cooper, Lane. *Greek Genius and Its Influence.* Ithaca: Cornell University Press, 1952.

Cornford, F. M. *Plato's Theory of Knowledge.* New York: Bobbs-Merrill, 1957.

———. *Before and After Socrates.* New York: Cambridge University Press, 1960.

Cryer, N. S., Jr. and Vayhinger, John M., eds. *Casebook in Pastoral Counseling.* Nashville: Abingdon Press, 1962.

Daane, James. *The Freedom of God.* Grand Rapids: Eerdmans Publishing Co., 1973.

Daiches, David, and Thorlby, Anthony, eds. *The Classical World.* Literature and Western Civilization, vol. 1. London: Aldus House, 1972.

De Graaf, Arnold H. "Toward an Integral Model of Psychotherapy." *The Bulletin* 6:3 (1980).

The Detroit Magazine. *Detroit Free Press,* April 14, 1974.

Dicks, Russell L. *Pastoral Work and Personal Counseling.* New York: The Macmillan Co., 1949.

———. *Toward Health and Wholeness.* New York: The Macmillan Co., 1980.

Dubos, René. *Beast or Angel? Choices That Make Us Human.* New York: Charles Scribner's Sons, 1974.

Eliade, M. *Yoga: Immortality and Freedom.* Tr. by Willard R. Trask. New York: Pantheon Books, 1958.

———. *Cosmos and History.* Tr. by Willard R. Trask. New York: Harper & Brothers, 1959.

Ellens, J. H. "Anxiety and the Rise of Religious Experience." *JPT* 3:1 (Winter 1975).

———. "Anxiety and Religion." *CAPS Proceedings,* 1974.

———. "Creative Worship." *CAPS Proceedings,* 1970.

———. "Biblical Themes in Psychological Theory and Practice." *The Bulletin* of CAPS 6:2 (1980).

———. "The Church and the Metropolis." *Missiology,* March 1975.

———. "The Christian Concept of Man and the Humanities," "Concepts of Self in Christian Experience and Psychotherapy," "Humanization of Man in the Antique World," "Concepts of the Self in Biblical Theology." Papers read at the Society of Biblical Literature and Exegesis, 1979.

———. "Communication and Christian Anthropology." Paper read at the Society of Biblical Literature and Exegesis.

———. "Communication Theory and Petitionary Prayer." *JPT* 5:1 (Winter 1977).

———. "Issues in Premarital Sexuality." *The Bulletin* of CAPS 2:2 (1976).

———. "Liturgical Leadership and Psychological Response Patterns." *CAPS* Proceedings, 1973.

———. "The Problem of Evil." *The Orb: A Journal of Religious Affairs* (Winter 1974).

———. "Psychological Dynamics in Christian Worship." *JPT* 1:4 (October 1973).

————. "A Theology of Communication." *JPT* 2:2 (Spring 1974).

————. "A Theology of Humanness and Christian Psychotherapy." Paper read at the CAPS Convention 1976.

————. "Psychological Process and Christian Experience in Psychotherapy." In *Research in Mental Health and Religious Behavior,* edited by W. J. Donaldson, Jr. Atlanta: PSI, 1976.

Ellis, Peter. *The Yahwist: The Bible's First Theologian.* Notre Dame, Ind.: Fides Publishers, 1968.

Farnsworth, Kirk. "Embodied Integration." *JPT* 2:2 (Spring 1974).

Feder, Lillian. *Crowell's Handbook of Classical Literature.* New York: Thomas Y. Crowell, 1964.

Ferguson, John. *Utopias of the Classical World.* Ithaca: Cornell University Press, 1975.

Finch, John G. *The Message of Anxiety.* Taped lecture, CAPS Convention, 1976.

Fleck, J. Roland, and Carter, John D. *Psychology and Christianity: Integrative Readings.* Nashville: Abingdon, 1981.

Frankl, Viktor E. *Man's Search for Himself.* New York: Washington Square Press, 1963.

————. *The Doctor and the Soul.* 2d exp. ed. Tr. by Richard and Clara Winston. London: Souvenir Press Ltd., 1969.

Frazer, Sir James George. *New Golden Bough.* Ed. by T. Gaster. New York: Criterion, 1959.

Freud, Sigmund. *New Introductory Lectures on Psychoanalysis.* Tr. and ed. by James Strachey. New York: W. W. Norton & Co., 1965.

Fromm, Eric. *Psychoanalysis and Religion.* New Haven: Yale University Press, 1950.

————. *The Heart of Man.* New York: Harper & Row, 1964.

————. *The Anatomy of Human Destructiveness.* New York: Holt, Rinehart and Winston, 1973.

Gaster, Theodor. *Myth, Legend, and Custom in the Old Testament.* New York: Harper & Row, 1969.

Grand, Michael. *The Ancient Mediterranean.* New York: Charles Scribner's Sons, 1969.

Grene, David, and Lattimore, Richmond. *Aeschylus.* The Complete Greek Tragedies, vol. 1. Chicago: University of Chicago Press, 1970.

————. *Euripedes.* The Complete Greek Tragedies, vols. 3 & 4. Chicago: University of Chicago Press, 1970.

Grene, Marjorie. *A Portrait of Aristotle.* Chicago: University of Chicago Press, 1967.

Guthrie, W. K. C. *In The Beginning: Some Greek Views on the Origins of Life and the Early State of Man.* Ithaca: Cornell University Press, 1965.
————. *Greeks and Their Gods.* Boston: Beacon Press, 1968.
————. *Socrates.* New York: Cambridge University Press, 1971.
————. *The Sophists.* New York: Cambridge University Press, 1971.
Hall, Calvin S. *A Primer of Freudian Psychology.* New York: Mentor, 1961.
Hall, Calvin S., and Lindzey, Gardner. *Theories of Personality.* 3rd ed. New York: John Wiley & Sons, 1978.
Hamilton, Edith. *Mythology.* New York: Grosset & Dunlap, 1963.
————. *The Greek Way.* New York: W. W. Norton & Co., 1964.
————. *The Roman Way.* New York: W. W. Norton & Co., 1964.
Harriman, P. L. *New Dictionary of Psychology.* Philosophical Library. New York: McLeod, 1947.
Hawkes, Jacquetta. *Dawn of the Gods.* New York: Random House, 1968.
Hesiod. *Theogony.* Tr. by Norman O. Brown. New York: Bobbs-Merrill, 1953.
Hiltner, Seward. *Pastoral Counseling.* Nashville: Abingdon Press, 1949.
Hiltner, Seward, and Menninger, Karl, eds. *Constructive Aspects of Anxiety.* Nashville: Abingdon Press, 1963.
Homer. *The Complete Works of Homer.* New York: Random House, 1950.
Horney, Karen. *Neurotic Personality of Our Time.* New York: W. W. Norton & Co., 1937.
Jaeger, Werner. *Paideia: The Ideals of Greek Culture.* Tr. by Gilbert Highet. 3 vols. New York: Oxford University Press, 1945.
Jaki, Stanley L. *The Road of Science and the Ways to God.* Chicago: University of Chicago Press, 1978.
James, William. *Varieties of Religious Experience.* London: Longmans Green Ltd., 1911.
The Jerusalem Bible. Garden City, N. Y.: Doubleday & Co., 1966 and 1970.
Johnson, Paul E. *Psychology of Religion.* Rev. and enl. ed. Nashville: Abingdon Press, 1959.
————. *Psychology and Religion.* New Haven: Yale University Press, 1938.
Jung, C. G. *Undiscovered Self.* Tr. by R. F. C. Hull. Boston: Little, Brown, 1958.

147

————. *Man and His Symbols.* Garden City, N.Y.: Doubleday & Co., 1964.

Kant, I. *Critique of Pure Reason.* Tr. by Norman Kemp Smith. New York: The Macmillan Co., 1929.

————. *Critique of Practical Reason.* Tr. by Lewis White Beck. Library of Liberal Arts, no. 52. New York: Liberal Arts Press, 1956.

Kierkegaard, Søren. *Fear and Trembling/The Sickness unto Death.* Tr. by Walter Lowrie. Garden City, N.Y.: Doubleday & Co., 1954.

————. *Concept of Dread.* 2d ed. Tr. by Walter Lowrie. Princeton: Princeton University Press, 1957.

Kirk, G. S. *Homer and the Epic.* New York: Cambridge University Press, 1965.

Kitto, H. D. F. *The Greeks.* Baltimore: Penguin, 1957.

Klausner, Joseph. *From Jesus to Paul.* Tr. by William F. Stinespring. Boston: Beacon Press, 1961.

Koteskey, R. L. *Psychology from a Christian Perspective.* Nashville: Abingdon, 1980.

————. "Reaction: Theory or Data." *JPT* 8:3 (Fall 1980).

Landis, Carney, and Bolles, Marjorie M. *Textbook of Abnormal Psychology.* Rev. Ed. New York: The Macmillan Co., 1950.

Larzelere, Robert E. "The Task Ahead: Six Levels of Integration of Christianity and Psychology." *JPT* 8:1 (Spring 1980).

Lévêque, Pierre. *The Greek Adventure.* Tr. by Miriam Kochan. New York: World Publishing Co., 1968.

Linn, Louis, and Schwarz, Leo. *Psychiatry and Religious Experience.* New York: Random House, 1958.

Machen, J. Gresham. *Origin of Paul's Religion.* New York: The Macmillan Co., 1928.

MacKay, Donald. *The Clock Work Image: A Christian Perspective on Science.* Downers Grove, Ill.: Inter-Varsity Press, 1974.

Maddi, Salvatore R., ed. *Personality Theories: A Comparative Analysis.* 4th ed. Homewood, Ill.: The Dorsey Press, 1980.

Marron, H. I. *Education in Antiquity.* New York: Mentor, 1964.

Maslow, Abraham. *Motivation and Personality.* New York: Harper & Brothers, 1954.

Mathisen, Kenneth. "Back to Basics: A Broad Conceptual Model for the Integration of Psychology and Theology." *JPT* 8:3 (Fall 1980).

May, Rollo. *Meaning of Anxiety.* New York: Ronald Press, 1950.

————. *Psychology and the Human Dilemma*. New York: Van Nostrand Reinhold Co., 1967.

————. *Love and Will*. New York: W. W. Norton & Co., 1969.

————. *The Courage to Create*. New York: W. W. Norton & Co., 1975.

McLemore, Clinton W. "The Nature of Psychotheology: Varieties of Conceptual Integration." *JPT* 4:3 (Summer 1976).

McNeill, Robert. *God Wills Us Free*. New York: W. W. Norton & Co., 1975.

Mertz, Barbara. *Red Land, Black Land*. New York: Coward, McCann & Geoghegan, 1966.

Morford, Mark P. O., and Lenardon, Robert J. *Classical Mythology*. New York: David McKay Co., 1971.

Murray, Gilbert. *Five Stages of Greek Religion*. 3d ed. Garden City, N.Y.: Doubleday & Co., 1955.

Nouwen, Henri. *The Wounded Healer: Ministry in Contemporary Society*. New York: McGraw-Hill Book Co., 1975.

Orlebeke, Clifton, J. "Donald MacKay's Philosophy of Science." *Christian Scholars Review* 7:1 (1977).

Ornstein, Robert E. *The Psychology of Consciousness*. New York: Freeman, 1972.

Otto, Rudolf. *Idea of the Holy*. Tr. by John W. Harvey. New York: Oxford University Press, 1958.

Plato. *Great Dialogues of Plato*. New York: Mentor Books, 1960.

Punt, Neil. *Unconditional Good News: Toward an Understanding of Biblical Universalism*. Grand Rapids: Eerdmans Publishing Co., 1980.

Ramsay, W. M. *Cities of St. Paul*. Grand Rapids: Baker Book House, 1960.

Redding, David A. *The Couch and the Altar*. Philadelphia: J. B. Lippincott Co., 1968.

Restak, Richard M. *The Brain: The Last Frontier*. Garden City, N. Y.: Doubleday & Co., 1979.

Ridderbos, H. N. *Paul and Jesus*. Tr. by David H. Freeman. Grand Rapids: Baker Book House, 1958.

————. *Paul*. Tr. by J. Richard DeWitt. Grand Rapids: Eerdmans Publishing Co., 1975.

Robertson, A. T. *Paul's Joy in Christ*. Rev. and ed. by W. C. Strickland. Nashville: Broadman Press, 1959.

Ruch, Floyd L. *Psychology and Life*. 3d ed. Glenview, Ill.: Scott, Foresman and Co., 1948.

Runestam, Arvid. *Psychoanalysis and Christianity*. Rev. ed. Tr. by Oscar Winfield. Rock Island: Augustana, 1958.

Schaeffer, Francis A. *Escape from Reason*. Downers Grove, Ill.: Inter-Varsity Press, 1968.

———. *True Spirituality*. Wheaton: Tyndale House, 1972.

———. *Genesis in Space and Time*. Downers Grove, Ill.: Inter-Varsity Press, 1972.

Schleiermacher, F. *The Christian Faith*. Ed. by H. R. Mackintosh and J. S. Stewart. 2 vols. New York: Harper & Row, 1963.

Schuurman, Egbert. *Reflections of the Technological Society*. Toronto: Wedge, 1980.

———. *Technology and the Future: A Philosophical Challenge*. New York: Radix Books, 1980.

Shorey, Paul. *What Plato Said*. Chicago: University of Chicago Press, 1967.

Siegler, Miriam, and Osmond, Humphrey. *Models of Madness, Models of Medicine*. New York: The Macmillan Co., 1974.

Simon, Bennett. *Mind and Madness in Ancient Greece*. Ithaca: Cornell University Press, 1978.

Singer, June. *Boundaries of the Soul*. Garden City, N. Y.: Doubleday & Co., 1972.

Smith, Morton. *The Ancient Greeks*. Ithaca: Cornell University Press, 1970.

Smith, .T. V., ed. *From Thales to Plato*. Chicago: University of Chicago Press, 1968.

Standal, Stanley W., and Corsini, Raymond J., eds. *Critical Incidents in Psychotherapy*. Englewood Cliffs, N.J.: Prentice-Hall, 1959.

Stobart, J. C. *The Glory That Was Greece*. 4th ed., rev. by R. J. Hopper. New York: Hawthorne Books, 1964.

Thornton, Edward E. *Theology and Pastoral Counseling*. Philadelphia: Fortress Press, 1967.

Tillich, Paul. *Protestant Era*. Tr. by James Luther Adams. Chicago: University of Chicago Press, 1948.

———. *Systematic Theology*. Vol. 1. Chicago: University of Chicago Press, 1951.

———. *Meaning of Persons*. Tr. by Edwin Hudson. New York: Harper & Brothers, 1957.

Tournier, Paul. *Escape From Loneliness*. Tr. by John S. Gilmour. Philadelphia: The Westminster Press, 1962.

———. *Guilt and Grace*. Tr. by Arthur W. Heathcote et al. New York: Harper & Row, 1962.

————. *The Strong and The Weak.* Tr. by Edwin Hudson. Philadelphia: The Westminster Press, 1963.

Weatherhead, Leslie D. *Psychology, Religion, and Healing.* Nashville: Abingdon Press, 1952.

White, Robert W. *Abnormal Personality.* 2d ed. New York: Ronald Press, 1956.

Wolterstorff, Nicholas. *Reason Within the Bounds of Religion.* Grand Rapids: Eerdmans Publishing Co., 1976.

Index of Names

Index of Subjects and Scripture References